# SERGEANT CECIL

## THE IMPOSSIBLE DREAM:
## FROM RAGS TO RACING'S RICHES

### STEVE DENNIS

SPECIAL PHOTOGRAPHY BY EDWARD WHITAKER

highdown

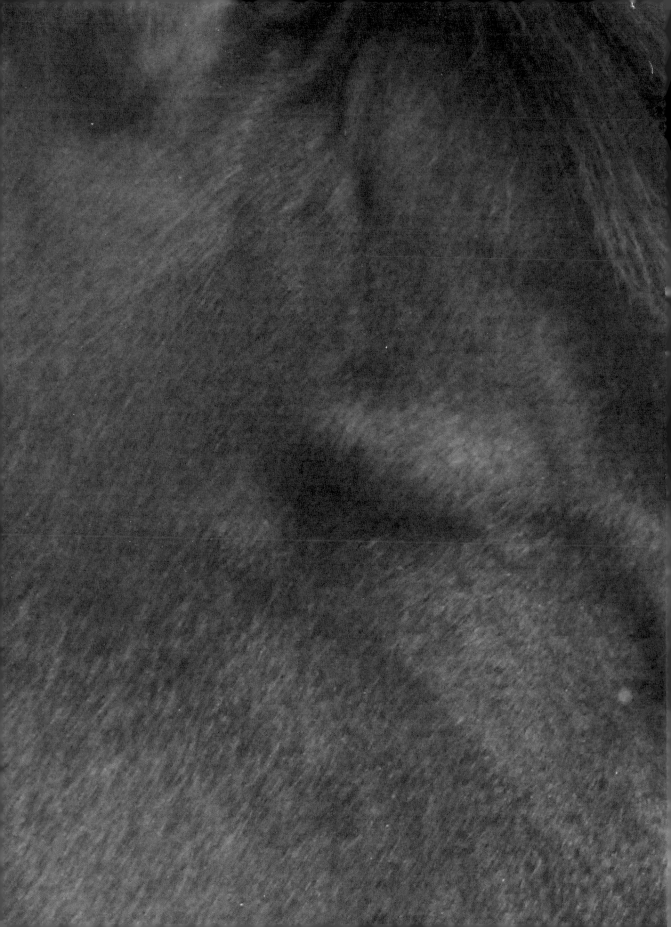

# SERGEANT CECIL

## THE IMPOSSIBLE DREAM:
## FROM RAGS TO RACING'S RICHES

## Acknowledgements

Special thanks must go to Terry Cooper, Rod Millman and Alan Munro, who gave
their valuable time and knowledge cheerfully and unstintingly, for without
their help this book would have been a much less interesting read. Also due
for praise are Seamus Mullins and Don Hazzard, who both provided a valuable
insight into Cecil's early days.

Brough Scott and the Raceform team, Jonathan Taylor, Julian Brown and
Adrian Morrish, deserve thanks for putting their trust in me to write the book and
for securing its passage from blank page to shiny hardback with patience and
practised expertise.

Edward Whitaker's superlative photography lifted the book to another level,
while John Hopkins' proof-reading safety net has made it look like I know
exactly what I'm talking about. Finally, thanks to Clare for curbing any
excesses with careful quality control and to Dax for letting me get on with
writing and not minding that he couldn't play on the computer.

Steve Dennis 2007

Published in 2007 by Highdown
an imprint of Raceform Ltd
Compton, Newbury, Berkshire RG20 6NL

A catalogue record for this book is available from the British Library.

ISBN 978-1-905156-39-9

Designed by Adrian Morrish

Printed by Butler and Tanner

Frontispiece: Sergeant Cecil by Edward Whitaker

# CONTENTS

# PROLOGUE

There were thousands of them cheering his name. As Sergeant Cecil made his processional way from the course to the winner's enclosure at Longchamp, his path was flanked six or seven deep by those who had rushed from the grandstands to welcome him in. His chestnut coat gleamed in the thin autumn sunshine and he walked through the crowd without turning a hair of it.

The man on his back was more animated. Frankie Dettori wore a wider smile than usual and seemed slightly overawed by the warmth of the welcome. The Italian had enjoyed big-race wins in all corners of the world, but there was something about this victory that he recognised as special. He pointed down at his mount as they walked in, emphasising that on this occasion the praise should be solely for the horse, that the jockey had just been along for the ride and had relished every second.

As horse and jockey entered the tree-lined paddock they were greeted by another throng, cheering, clapping, whistling, and not a few with tears in their eyes. As Sue Davey led Sergeant Cecil into the place reserved for the winner, where trainer Rod Millman and owner Terry Cooper were waiting, Dettori performed one of his hallmark flying dismounts and the roar of the crowd rose a notch. For Cooper, it was an emotional moment. He said: "I was dumbfounded - I didn't know whether to laugh or cry. As he came into the paddock, pricking his ears and nodding his head to the crowd, I said to myself 'Cooper, that's your little boy there'. It took a long time to sink in, what he'd achieved."

The race was the Prix du Cadran, the most prestigious staying race in France, staged on one of the greatest days in the world racing calendar. The Prix de l'Arc de Triomphe, always run on the first Sunday in October, was the highlight of the afternoon, but the supporting card was of the highest quality and the Cadran was the first big event. On Arc day, the Paris track is always overrun by British racegoers, who outnumber their hosts by two to one, and the 2006 renewal was no exception. They had crossed the Channel in their thousands to watch the cream of Europe's sprinters in the five-furlong Prix de l'Abbaye, the best European two-year-olds in the Prix Marcel Boussac and the Prix Jean-Luc Lagardere, and, of course, the Arc, the greatest middle-distance race in Europe.

The Cadran was scheduled to be the *hors d'oeuvre* to this great feast, but for many it was the centrepiece. They had travelled to Longchamp to see whether a cheaply bred, cheaply bought gelding, trained far from the madding crowd in the Devon countryside and owned not by a sheikh or a shipping tycoon but by a man who makes his money from selling office furniture, could add yet another glorious chapter to a story that had, in its playing out over the previous five years, captured the imagination of the racing world.

It was a story that had its roots in humble beginnings - the hero being seemingly neither marked out for fame nor fortune and, in his formative years, doing little to suggest that his destiny would be anything other than unremarkable, a foot-soldier in the footnotes of life's great library. There are similar billions out there whose tales are never told.

So how did our hero lift himself above the ordinary and into the extraordinary in the best traditions of a Hollywood epic? How did he go from *The Diary of a Nobody* to *The Greatest Story Ever Told*? How did he get from where he started to where he finds himself now, the cynosure of the masses, the name on everyone's lips, the star of the show?

Before he changed for his next ride, while the feeling was still intense, Dettori gave interviews for the reporters. They asked him what it was like, how the race went, how did it feel to win, what it was like to ride Sergeant Cecil. He answered their questions, and at the end, before turning away, summed up the whole situation in six simple words. He said: "What a horse. What a story."

*Cecil*

CHAPTER ONE

# IN THE
# BEGINNING

Jadidh, Cecil's dam, in contemplative mood

The story of Sergeant Cecil started on the afternoon of May 2, 1999, when he emerged into the world, just a bit of red fluff with long, unwieldy legs, in a field in Dorset. History doesn't record the thoughts of his mother, the mare Jadidh, but she had at least done the decent thing by giving birth at a convenient time.

The majority of mares give birth during the night, a throwback to the days when a birth-wet foal was a convenient snack for any passing predator, and a night delivery afforded the new arrival a few hours to find his feet and his wits before dawn. It was an unremarkable birth, straightforward and safe, and Arthur Barrow, on foaling duty and no doubt delighted that the mare had chosen a civilised hour to produce her first-born, rubbed the new arrival down with a handful of straw, checked him for obvious imperfections and, finding none, left mare and foal to get on with life.

Barrow had his own place in racing's record books as the trainer of classy chaser Master Smudge, awarded the 1980 Cheltenham Gold Cup on the belated disqualification of Tied Cottage. He had also trained horses for Don Hazzard, the breeder of Sergeant Cecil - "I couldn't have had a nicer fellow for a trainer," says Hazzard - and although his association with Sergeant Cecil was brief, he played an important role. When they were ready to travel, he took mare and foal back

The young Cecil

Quiet time in the tackroom

to Hazzard's place in Mere, where they were turned out into the Dorset spring sunshine.

Sergeant Cecil was a late foal, which is considered a disadvantage for a thoroughbred. Thoroughbreds have two birthdays, just like the Queen, and the official and most important one falls on January 1, when all thoroughbreds become a year older. The ideal, therefore, is to have a foal born as soon after the beginning of January as possible, as it will then have a full year to develop before becoming a yearling. The covering season starts on February 14, when the irony of it also being Valentine's Day is overlooked as stallions and mares across the northern hemisphere begin the procreative production line. Eleven months later, or thereabouts, and the clatter of tiny hooves is heard.

The later the foal, the more it will be at a disadvantage when starting its racing career. A January foal has four months' growth over a May foal, which is a considerable amount among immature specimens. Many race as two-year-olds before actually reaching their second birthday. As thoroughbreds mature, the difference becomes negligible to the point of vanishing. Sergeant Cecil's natural birthday might have held him back had he been bred to be a precocious two-

Don Hazzard with Jadidh in her racing days

11

year-old, but his pedigree hinted otherwise and Hazzard was well aware that his new racehorse was likely to take time to develop.

Hazzard, 72 when Sergeant Cecil was foaled, had owned racehorses for about 18 years and had had around a dozen winners with a variety of trainers before buying Jadidh at Tattersalls Sales in Newmarket. A nurseryman and plant grower by trade, he forged his path the hard way after his father, a veteran of the Great War, died when his son was just two years of age. He left school at the age of 14 and within two weeks was working as a motor engineer earning ten shillings a week. His marriage to Janet in 1958 prompted the switch from engines to plants, as his bride's family was in the nursery business.

Well known on the west country circuit and a regular fixture at Wincanton and Salisbury, Hazzard adopts a hands-on approach to racehorse ownership. "No-one trained one of my horses unless I could go into the weighing room and pick up the saddle, saddle the horse and give the jockey a leg-up," he says with a laugh in his rich country brogue.

"That nearly killed me once at Uttoxeter, though, as my jockey, Sophie Mitchell, barely weighed 8st but the horse had 11st 7lb on its back. The saddle was full of lead and, let me tell you, it's a long way from the weighing room to the parade ring at Uttoxeter. It seemed even further that day."

His can-do attitude again came to the fore when he and his friend Nicky Dawe,

Jadidh on the way to victory

On the way to the gallops

husband of Somerset trainer Jackie, went to the Autumn sales in Newmarket in 1991. Self-confessedly a buyer of cheap horses, he was disappointed to discover that his pocket wouldn't stretch to the vast majority of horses going through the sale ring. Like the canny countryman he is, however, he bided his time and, by half past seven, the place was almost empty. Going through the ring at that time were horses from the local Newmarket yards, well-bred cast-offs being offloaded to make room for the next intake of yearlings. There are many bargains to be found in these consignments, horses who have either failed to cope with the hurly-burly of life in a big yard or who have been slow to develop and need more time, an indulgence that the richest owners are usually unwilling to grant.

Jadidh fell into the second category having run just once, showing a modicum of promise when runner-up in a Yarmouth maiden for trainer Alec Stewart, who had made his reputation with the mighty Mtoto, winner of two Eclipse Stakes and a King George before finishing an unlucky runner-up in the Prix de l'Arc de Triomphe three years earlier. Jadidh was owned by Hamdan Al-Maktoum, one of the four incredibly rich and incredibly successful Maktoum brothers who have dominated British racing since the early 1980s, who that season had enjoyed success at the highest level with 1,000 Guineas winner Shadayid. He evidently - and understandably - saw no need to hang on to a stoutly bred filly who had run just once, so she, among others from Stewart's yard, was packed off to the sales in the hope that she would catch someone's eye. Jadidh caught Hazzard's eye and, as you might expect, the hands-on operator did the bidding himself - not that there was very much of it. The hammer fell at 2,800gns, and Hazzard had another horse.

Jadidh was well bred, as you might expect of a horse bred by a sheikh at his own private stud, Derrinstown Stud in Ireland. An April foal, she was by 1982 St Leger winner Touching Wood, a son of 1972 Derby hero Roberto, out of Petrol, a daughter of 1979 Derby winner Troy.

Touching Wood, although a Classic winner, was not a great success at stud, his best offspring being Ascot Gold Cup winner Ashal and Doncaster Cup winner Great Marquess, although he did also sire Pertemps Network, who won eight times over hurdles in his novice season. That kind of record tends to lead to an abrupt exile from the established breeding centres, and in Touching Wood's case he was 'deported' to New Zealand in 1988, where he took up

stallion duties at Fayette Park Stud at a fee of $3,000 before being pensioned off in 1999.

Petrol hailed from a reasonably speedy family and won over a mile as a three-year-old. Jadidh was her third foal and her second by Touching Wood. Her later foals were by sires with more speed than her earlier mates, and her most able offspring was her last, the classy handicapper Refuse To Lose, who won six races including the Royal Hunt Cup at Royal Ascot.

The input of Touching Wood spelled stamina, not speed, and it should have come as no surprise that Jadidh was a late developer who didn't make her debut until late July of her three-year-old season, in the aforementioned Yarmouth maiden over a mile and three-quarters. She finished runner-up in a field of four, beaten comfortably by a filly called Marie de France, who had never won before and would never win again. Little wonder that she ended up at the sales.

Hazzard saw possibilities for his new purchase, but not on the Flat. That November, now trained by Jackie Dawe, she made her debut in Hazzard's yellow and dark blue colours in a three-year-old hurdle at Nottingham, ridden by Nicky. She ran a fair race and, a week later, went down the road to Exeter and won a selling hurdle worth almost £1,500. Hazzard had made a swift return on his investment.

He says: "I spoke to Alec Stewart's head lad at Salisbury the following year, and he said that she was such a small filly that they only put the lightest riders on her, and they couldn't believe that within a fortnight of being sold she was running over hurdles under 10st 7lb.

"After that Exeter seller we had to look sharp and buy her back, and just as well we did. She won six races for me and was placed many times, let alone what she did after she finished racing."

Jadidh raced 65 times for Hazzard over the next five years, generally in low grade races and at west country tracks such as Newton Abbot, Taunton and Wincanton, on occasion acquitting herself well in defeat against a rising star. The young conditional jockey Darren Salter - now a driving instructor - formed an enduring alliance with her, and Hazzard did his best to put the two together as Jadidh moved base from Jackie Dawe to Chris Wildman at the end of 1993, and from Wildman to Arthur Barrow for her 1996-97 campaign, before closing out her career at the end of 1997 when in the care of Paul Ritchens.

Her finest hour came in February 1995, when ploughing through the mud at Sandown to win a conditional jockeys' hurdle over two and three-quarter miles. She was tough and game - so tough that Hazzard conceived a plan to run her twice in one afternoon at Lingfield. He was only thwarted when her first race was divided and she was scheduled to run in the second division, the third race on the card. As her second engagement was in the fifth race, even Hazzard had to concede that it might be stretching her good nature too far to run twice in the space of an hour - and the stewards fined him £300 for his audacity.

Her time on the track came to an end when she broke a blood vessel at Fontwell in

December 1997. Hazzard called it quits, and looks back on that successful bid at Tattersalls as the best move he ever made. Not only did his mare win him ten times as much in prize-money than she initially cost, but he got unbeatable fun out of her in the process and now had a potential broodmare with whom to have a bit more.

The phrase bandied around by those in the racing world to illustrate the mechanics of thoroughbred breeding is 'breed the best to the best and hope for the best'. If you are the Aga Khan, or John Magnier, all well and good. But that old saw only applies in 98 per cent of cases if the wording is changed to 'breed whatever you have to whatever you can afford and reconcile yourself to impending disappointment and/or financial ruin'.

Most people with a broodmare do exactly what Hazzard did - take proximity as the main imperative and choose the stallion up the road, whatever his suitability and previous record at stud. However, Hazzard had both proximity and science on his side as he selected Jadidh's first mate.

"It was pure luck that I chose King's Signet," he says, his self-deprecation concealing a well-formulated plan. "I knew I had a good distance horse with a pedigree full of stamina, so I wanted to put some speed into her. King's Signet had been a good sprinter and was at Blackmore Vale Stud in Gillingham, just down the road. He was advertised for £3,000, but I got him for £2,500 because Jadidh was a winning mare."

King's Signet was a sprinter through and through. His dam was the brilliantly fast French filly Sigy, winner of the Prix de l'Abbaye, and his sire was the extremely successful stallion Nureyev, a son of Northern Dancer and first past the post in the 1980 2,000 Guineas before being disqualified. During a celebrated career at stud, Nureyev sired champions such as Theatrical, Miesque, Zilzal, Peintre Celebre, Spinning World and Reams Of Verse.

King's Signet, a bright chestnut half-brother to Sicyos, another high-class sprinter,

17

was trained by John Gosden for Sheikh Mohammed and was himself a very late developer, not making his racecourse debut until August of his three-year-old career, when well beaten in a Goodwood maiden.

That was over seven furlongs, a trip he would never be asked to tackle again, and on his next outing, at Thirsk over six furlongs, he gave the first intimation of his speed and class when thrashing an admittedly weak field by eight lengths and more. He won next time out too, at Yarmouth, but was beaten on his last three outings of the season.

However, on his belated reintroduction as a four-year-old, he won the exceedingly competitive Gosforth Park Cup at Newcastle in June, which set him up nicely for the valuable and historic Stewards' Cup at Glorious Goodwood the following month. This six-furlong handicap always attracts a field of around 30 and rewards spectators with the sight of an old-fashioned cavalry charge thundering down the straight course at British racing's most picturesque track. King's Signet, ridden by Willie Carson, was a 16-1 chance and for many his hopes of winning were scuppered by top weight of 9st 10lb. Those whose faith was unshaken were rewarded when Carson brought King's Signet up the far side of the track to beat Hard To Figure by a length and a half. It was a superb performance, and one that far

Willie Carson in the winner's enclosure at Goodwood

King's Signet wins the Stewards' Cup

outshone his final success when dead-heating with Marina Park in the Listed Scarbrough Stakes at Doncaster.

As a stallion, King's Signet - like Touching Wood - was not a success, his only other performer of note besides Sergeant Cecil being the Listed-winning sprinter Bali Royal. Like Touching Wood, he too was banished, in his case to Saudi Arabia. In *Flat Horses of 2005*, Janet Hickman wrote of King's Signet: "He had a very modest record overall from limited chances."

So what Hazzard did was breed a staying hurdler to a sprinter who was low in the estimation of the bloodstock world and whose record of successful offspring was very short and not particularly sweet. Breed the best to the best and hope for the best?

Sergeant Cecil was the result, the latest heir to the ages of thoroughbred breeding. His heritage stretches back more than 300 years to the three Arab stallions who are regarded as the fathers of all thoroughbreds - the Darley Arabian, the Byerley Turk and the Godolphin Barb. The first-named has developed into the foremost influence in modern racing with the most dominant line, stretching back through the great Canadian nonpareil Northern Dancer to Eclipse, the greatest horse of the 18th century. Sergeant Cecil traces back along that line in his turn through both Northern Dancer and Roberto, his great-grandsires.

## "He got himself a real bargain"

But for now, the fingerprints of history were of less importance than eating summer grass and growing up. The horse who would later be named Sergeant Cecil spent the rest of his first year with Hazzard, being carefully looked after by Pauline Berry, who worked at the nursery for Hazzard's son Clive and loved her part-time job of caring for the little chestnut.

Jadidh had been covered again shortly after producing Sergeant Cecil, this time by

Blandford Forum

Busy Flight, and she gave birth to another colt the following May. He would eventually be called Jayer Gilles, and Berry looked after him too until a dispute at work led to her leaving her job and moving away. Hazzard was unable to look after the mare, foal at foot and yearling, so he cast about for a solution. One was found for Jadidh and Jayer Gilles in the shape of neighbour Tony Brimble, who paid £1,200 for mare and foal. Jayer Gilles was even slower to come to hand than his dam, and it wasn't until the summer of his four-year-old career that he made his debut. At the time of writing, after 19 more races, he has yet to get off the mark.

The future Sergeant Cecil, however, had still to find a billet, but sanctuary was at hand in the shape of Terry Cooper, who ran an office furniture company in nearby Blandford Forum. Cooper and Hazzard were friends, having met a couple of years earlier when Cooper was looking for a horse to hack around on. He answered an ad placed by Hazzard for a mountain of a horse called Hazzard's Boy, but he was not what Cooper was looking for. However, there was another, more suitable horse available and Cooper bought that instead. He had a new horse and a new friend. The first link in the chain had been forged.

Cooper had already had a couple of horses in training and was looking for another, so Hazzard asked him to have a look at the chestnut yearling. Cooper liked him, and struck a deal with Hazzard to pay £1,000 down, with an extra £400 payable if the horse won two races. Although in hindsight it is the sort of deal to make the seller rend his clothes in anguish, Hazzard has no regrets.

Terry Cooper with his new purchase

"At the time, I couldn't cope with the horses, so I was pleased to sell them on," he says. "The mare has obviously increased considerably in value after all Sergeant Cecil's exploits, and Terry got himself a real bargain, didn't he - but that's the way it can go when you breed racehorses." Such a phlegmatic and genuine approach is wholly in character, and although Hazzard sold his yearling for a song he still takes a great deal of enjoyment from his part in the story and from the achievements of Sergeant Cecil.

So the little colt had his first change of scenery, leaving his mother behind and making his first move out into the world, travelling about 20 miles across the rolling Dorset countryside to Paradise. Now, most of us must find our way to paradise by way of Kensal Green, but Sergeant Cecil took a more picturesque route: by horsebox down the twisting country roads to Neville Poole's Paradise Farm Stud. Poole is another wise old countryman in the mould of Hazzard and as a breeder has had a fair amount of success in recent years, notably with Diomed Stakes winner Hazyview and Coventry Stakes winner Hellvelyn.

Cooper, who lives a mile or two up the road and is another whose voice betrays his western roots, says: "I knew Neville by sight but no more than that.

A little bit of work in the sunshine

However, I had to find somewhere for my yearling to stay, so I approached him to see if he had room. He did, and I was delighted that the horse could be so close to where I lived and also with someone who clearly knew a lot about horses and had had plenty of success with the ones he bred."

Paradise Farm Stud is set in fine chalk grassland, ideal conditions for growing racehorses to develop bone and strength, and the ideal place for the yearling in the months leading up to the day he went into training. But before that day came he needed to lose something and gain something.

The loss was a swift procedure and caused him little discomfort. Bred as humbly as he was, the colt was thought unlikely to make a top-class Flat racer, and Cooper had it in mind that he might find his niche over hurdles. Furthermore, there were mares and fillies on the stud who neither wanted nor needed the amorous attentions of a randy yearling. There were few pros and many cons to the question of the colt's testicles, and to that end the vet was called to perform a gelding operation on the youngster. What you don't know you've had, you don't miss. Without unnecessary hormones addling his brain, he would be much more amenable to life as a racehorse and, without the sexual imperative bubbling through his veins, his career would be prolonged far beyond the brief here-today-and-gone-tomorrow of the lucky few destined for the breeding shed and the pages of the *Stud Book*.

Now the little chestnut gelding needed a name. The naming of racehorses is a dangerous game, just as vital to get right as the naming of a child. For every Bold Ruler, Nijinsky and Allez France there is a Son Of Sharp Shot (a son of Sharp Shot, necessarily), Transvestite (heaven only knows) or Geary's Cold Rolled (Mr Geary was a steel tycoon). Get it right, and racefans and headline-writers the world over will warm to you, get it wrong and you've wasted a glorious opportunity. Many horses are named in connection with the name of their sire or dam, or both, and if Cooper had followed this method he might have chosen Touching Jade, or Jadidh's First, or Wood Effect, or some equally unmemorable construction. However, he had something much more satisfactory in mind, and tells the story well.

"My father died when I was nine, and my poor mother was left without any money and two children to bring up," he says. "As a result, we couldn't give dad a headstone, we couldn't afford it, and although it wasn't something that worried me greatly when I was young and just skipping through life, as you get older you have more time to reflect on things.

"So when I got this little chap I thought it would be nice to name him after my father as a memorial. Dad served in the Great War in France and in the Second World War in England - he was Sergeant Cecil Edward Cooper. He enlisted at Camberwell in the Welsh Fusiliers in October 1915 and was assigned to the Machine-Gun Corps (no. 9859) the following year. He was sent out to France in July 1916, came back after two months, then went back out again in July 1917 and served there for a year.

"He finished the war as a corporal - it says in his army book 'conduct: exemplary' - and when the Second World War began he enlisted in the Hampshire Regiment and served in the National Defence Companies, rising to the rank of sergeant.

"So I thought I'd call the horse Sergeant Cecil - it's a good name, it sounds nice, it's easily shortened for a 'stable name', it's a proper name for a horse. Strangely enough - you might not believe this, but it's true - before we officially named him Sergeant Cecil, my daughter Sam nicknamed him Bob, because of course we had to have some kind of everyday name for convenience. Later on, my elder sister Jo told me that all my father's workmates called him Bob too - it's quite an eerie coincidence. I

certainly picked the right horse to give the right name to."

It was third time lucky and no mistake. Cooper's first horse was Silver Brief, who finished no closer than fourth in nine attempts for four different trainers, and his second was Honeyshan, who fared less well, finishing no better than sixth in seven starts on the Flat and over hurdles. Since that less than auspicious entry into ownership - Cooper describes it as "a waste of time" - he had kept only a watching brief until Hazzard piqued his interest with a chestnut yearling with a big white blaze and four white feet. He had let the registration of his colours lapse, and when he phoned Weatherbys to re-register them was told that someone else had pinched his colour scheme.

"My first horse, Silver Brief, was an iron grey, and I chose my colours to suit his coat. They were black with three large yellow spots, and a yellow cap with black spots," he says. "When I couldn't get them back, I decided to keep what I had and add yellow sleeves, and I think my new colours are nicer than my original ones - more distinctive."

Cooper had his colours and a horse to carry them - now he needed to find someone to train his horse. Perhaps wishing to make a clean break with the disappointments of the past, he decided to send Sergeant Cecil to a trainer he hadn't used before, and because Hazzard had already had horses at the yard he chose Seamus Mullins, just a few miles up the A303 near Amesbury. If Sergeant Cecil was to race as a two-year-old he needed to be taught to be a racehorse, so after the clocks went back and the Dorset days began to shorten, he was led up into another horsebox for the short journey to Mullins' yard. He was just over 18 months old, and his life was about to change again.

CHAPTER TWO

# A WORK IN PROGRESS

Seamus Mullins was a good choice of trainer for a horse who needed time to develop and mature. The Irishman, working from a yard practically in the shadow of Stonehenge, had many years of experience with horses, learning his trade at the knee of some of the biggest names in the business.

He started out with his uncle, Paddy Mullins, who was a legend in the training ranks even before he won both Champion Hurdle and Cheltenham Gold Cup with the much-loved mare Dawn Run in the mid-1980s. Mullins spent a season with his uncle before moving to Britain, the season Dawn Run was learning the ropes herself in bumpers, and Mullins narrowly missed the chance to ride the great mare on the racecourse. "I came quite close to riding her in a race once when her owner-rider, Charmian Hill, was delayed," he says. "But she arrived in time, and I didn't get another opportunity."

On his arrival in Britain, he benefited from time spent with Gold Cup-winning trainers Jimmy FitzGerald and Toby Balding as well as with Jim Old, and during his time with the last named saw the other side of the coin as far as Dawn Run was concerned. He says: "When Dawn Run won the Champion Hurdle I was working for Jim Old, who trained the runner-up Cima. I was the one Irishman at Cheltenham not screaming for the mare, although I was thrilled that she won for the family."

Mullins saw racing life from the back of a horse, too, riding as an amateur and winning the four-mile National Hunt Chase at the Cheltenham Festival in 1989 on the Balding-trained Boraceva. But riding was a distant runner-up to training as far as Mullins was

Seamus Mullins, wearing the
smile of a winning trainer

concerned, and he had charge of a successful string of point-to-pointers before taking out a public licence in 1992, later developing a reputation as a trainer predominantly of jumpers who put the individual requirements of his horses before anything else, never being afraid to give a horse time rather than attempting to cash in quickly with short-term gains.

He does evening stables himself, personally feeding every one of his horses between 9pm and 10pm, finding it the best time to learn a little more about their wellbeing and character. He told Rodney Masters, in an interview for the *Racing Post*: "It's my favourite time of the working day, just the horses and myself. I get to learn so much about them over this next hour or so. The way they stand when they're relaxed in the box, the way they approach the manger. Uncle Paddy told me some of the signs to look for, and I've picked up other clues along the way."

His approach would be vital to Sergeant Cecil's mental and physical growth. When he arrived, clattering down the ramp out of Neville Poole's horsebox, Mullins saw a small gelding, weak and immature, one who would require thoughtful and considered treatment to make the most of whatever talent he might be naturally equipped with. The little chestnut had come to the right place. Now known as just plain Cecil (because training stables are seldom respecters of rank), he was allotted a box in a corner of the main section of the yard and left to settle in.

The first step in any horse's education, whether it be a racer or a riding-school pony, is the breaking-in process. The niceties of political correctness haven't found too many footholds in the world of horseracing, and the term 'breaking in' could do with a makeover. In this world, breaking means making - and if the process is carried out calmly, considerately and in an unhurried manner, it will set a horse up for life.

Alison Dunford was set the task of breaking in Sergeant Cecil, and as befitted his lowly status he was just one among many that she worked on that winter for Mullins.

"You only remember the awkward ones," she says, "and I don't remember too much about him, so at least that shows he wasn't any trouble. I remember that he was quite quiet and fairly quick to break - he coped fine with the lunging, the work on the long reins, and being backed and ridden away. He was always straightforward, that's what I remember most."

After Sergeant Cecil had been 'tamed', he was ready to join the rest of the yard at work and build up slowly to the point where he was fit to run and fit to be seen on a racecourse. He spent his first couple of weeks just walking and trotting around the sand canter with one other horse for company, finding his feet and his place in the world, and then graduated up to the main gallop with the rest of the string. Mullins says: "He was always slightly weak, and I was never convinced at any stage that I had the finished article. When he was two, he never looked like a two-year-old, I always had the feeling he'd be better as a three-year-old. Of course, when he was three, I looked at him and saw a potential four-year-old - at that stage of his life he was never quite there."

It might have been the hangover of a late foaling date, or the pedigree that drew a line through 'precocity' and underlined 'patience', but Mullins always had the impression that Sergeant Cecil was a work in progress, a rough draft, a pencil sketch of the Sistine Chapel ceiling without all the fancy colouring-in done.

To Mullins, Sergeant Cecil was one of 40 or so horses with broadly similar needs, not special, far from it. When he wasn't actively looking at him or thinking about him, he receded into the background along with the rest of his stablemates. If Mullins was the headmaster of the equine academy, Lou Griffin was the motherly matron - she looked after Sergeant Cecil, brushed him, washed him, made his bed, mucked him out, talked to him when he was quiet, cheered him up when he was down, poured cold water on him when he got a bit above himself. She had to do a lot of that.

"He was very, very cheeky," she says. "Never nasty, not a bit of it, but very cocksure, very much the big 'I am'. When he was out with the rest of the string he'd be nibbling away at the bushes on the roadside, so you'd pull his head away and he'd start chewing at the knee of whoever was riding alongside. Then he'd whip round at the bottom of the gallops and cause more fuss. He was always doing something you'd want to stop him doing.

"He was as good as gold when it came to work, though, very straightforward. He liked to work, but he liked to mess about as well. I used to ride him two weeks on, two weeks off with a chap called Danny Allen, because neither one of us could face riding him all the time."

Before Sergeant Cecil came along, Griffin had looked after Jadidh at Chris Wildman's and Paul Ritchens' - "She was very laid-back and placid. You could do what you liked with her, she was a lovely old mare" - and she left Ritchens' yard she moved to work for Mullins, taking Don Hazzard with her as an owner. It was he who introduced Terry Cooper to Mullins, in one of racing's convoluted, circular pathways by which everyone seems connected. So Griffin knew the family, and was well aware that Sergeant Cecil's bolshie behaviour hadn't been handed down from Jadidh.

Mullins agreed, having had an unusual experience with another son of King's Signet, a character still fresh in the memory of his wife, Sally. She says: "We had one horse by that sire who thought he was a sheep. I think he only ran for us once, he wasn't any good, but his formative years as a foal and yearling were spent with sheep, so he thought he was one too. You could walk up to him and 'baa' like a sheep, and he'd come to you."

Mullins adds: "Cecil didn't get his dodgy attitude from his dam, because she was a sweet, honest mare. It's true, he was a bit of a brat at that stage. He was like a child sitting at the back of the class, always trying to get away with something.

"The other horses took an instant dislike to him, he was always annoying them when they were trying to be sensible and get their work done. He wanted to be top dog - if there was a commotion in the string you could guarantee that Cecil had started it."

## "He had his own ideas about everything"

"He had his own ideas about everything, it was as if he was questioning your methods. He would test your patience, he was very challenging. But if in turn I could challenge his mental attitude, I knew there'd be a racehorse in him," says Mullins. And nowhere did Sergeant Cecil test Mullins' patience more than when the time came to introduce him to starting stalls, in the summer of his two-year-old career.

Mullins is not an advocate of the 'big stick' approach, preferring to use soft words to coax and cajole his horses into doing what he wants. However, he was struggling with Sergeant Cecil when it came to putting him through the stalls. Getting him out when he was in was no problem, he'd jump out like an old hand, it was getting him in to start with that was proving the sticking point. Mullins concocted a plan.

He says: "There were a couple of mornings when we failed to get him in at all, and as he was approaching the time for a run it was something we needed to sort out. If we just left it up to the stalls handlers on the day of the race, we'd run the risk of him having a bad experience and taking against the whole thing, or not going in at all, which would have been embarrassing with the owner there, so I wanted to do something before he raced.

"I thought I'd get the experts in, so I had a word with a friend of mine and one morning in September four lads from the stalls-handling team turned up in a van to give Cecil a private lesson. But even that wasn't straightforward. They got him in twice, but they really had to work hard to get him in there. These were the pros, they were used to dealing with problems, but they were sweating buckets and he just stood there laughing at them, not turning a hair. He wasn't frightened - I'd say he'd never been frightened of anything in his life - he just thought 'this isn't for me'.

"When they left they told me not to bother trying to get him in again, but just said to let them know when and where he was going to run and they'd explain the situation to the handlers at the course that day. They seemed to think that once he'd done it on the track he'd be fine, and they were right - but if they hadn't come down in the first place he may never have gone in at all."

The trainer's individual approach was paying off. For all Sergeant Cecil's natural ebullience, he was being taught to do his job without being aware of the process. He still liked to manufacture his own routine - he was partial to a mid-afternoon nap, flat out on the floor of his box, and when Dunford or Griffin went in to groom him they didn't have the heart to wake him up and turn him over, so just brushed the half of him they could see - but he was slowly turning into a racehorse. Mullins schools all his horses over hurdles for a spot of extra education, and always thought the leggy, raw

Sergeant Cecil looked like he'd make a jumper, but he would start off on the Flat.

He says: "I'm not a man for blood tests and all that stuff. I'm an old-fashioned stockman, I judge a lot by eye, and when a horse looks well and is pleasing me I get on and race him." Sergeant Cecil was ready to race.

The stalls-handlers episode ushered in his first racecourse appearance. That morning he was entered for a mile maiden at Kempton five days hence, long before the course's transformation into an all-weather track, and Mullins booked a young jockey, the not particularly well-known Shashi Righton, for the ride. Not much was expected of him on his debut, it was purely a sighter to see how much he had learned and how much he had still to learn. There were 11 runners, and Sergeant Cecil was the complete outsider of the field at 100-1. That was hardly surprising, considering he had a trainer more associated with jump racing, was not bred to be a zippy two-year-old, and was taking on more experienced rivals. Whatever his perceived shortcomings, at least he looked the part - he was awarded the prize for the best-turned-out horse.

Cooper has a photograph of Sergeant Cecil going down to the start at Kempton (*see next page*). He is as shiny as a new penny but obviously weak and open to plenty of physical development. The comment in the racecard was unusually prescient - 'one to watch with the future in mind'.

He went into the stalls after a bit of persuasion from the handlers, forewarned no doubt by their colleagues, but missed the break entirely and it took some time

Cecil and Shashi Righton on the way to the start at Kempton for his first race

before the penny dropped and he realised what he was there for. Righton did a little pushing in the final quarter-mile and he kept on gamely to the line to finish eighth, beaten just over 11 lengths by the winner, Mananan McLir, who would go on to finish runner-up in the Grade 1 Hollywood Derby a little over a year later.

Cooper and Mullins were both pleased with the performance, Sergeant Cecil having shown an aptitude for the job after an understandably shaky start. With the end of the season approaching, he was entered for another maiden a week later, this time over two furlongs further at Bath. "The first run didn't take anything out of him," says Mullins, "and although to run a horse again quickly wouldn't be a thing I'd do a lot, the fact that the ground was beginning to turn, and because the owner was local and wanted to see his horse run, led to him having one more race before the end of the year."

The outcome was much the same as at Kempton. Griffin pocketed another best-turned-out award and Cecil, again a 100-1 chance, left the stalls on terms before dropping back with half a mile to run. Righton got him running again down the outside of the field a quarter of a mile out, and he stayed on all the way to the line through beaten horses for seventh, 11 lengths behind Stage By Stage. For the second time in two starts, he was going forwards, not backwards, at the finish.

Mullins says: "Hand on heart, I can honestly say that I was never disappointed with any of his runs. He was backward and weak and there was plenty of improvement to come physically. After each of his runs I could always see a future for him."

"Who am I riding today, guv'nor?"

Cooper, pleased that his youngster had finished his first season on an encouraging note, took him back to Paradise Farm Stud for the winter, while Mullins concentrated on his jumping string.

## "We never fell out over the horse"

Sergeant Cecil returned in the depths of winter and fitted neatly back into the routine he relished. After a few weeks working up the artificial gallop, from the top of which the ancient sarsen stones of Stonehenge are plainly visible on the other side of the A303, he was ready for a return to racecourse action. His debut as a three-year-old at Lingfield was to be his only outing on an all-weather surface, and one that was compromised by the antics of the filly in the neighbouring stall, who kicked up a right fuss next to our placid old stalls veteran, by now taking the loading procedure in his stride. He made little impression, again under Righton, until running on through the final furlong to finish ninth, but at least with a third run under his belt he had earned a handicap mark, which had been Mullins' main objective.

"You'll laugh, and I don't mind telling you," says Mullins, safe in the knowledge that his opinion has been rendered amusingly naïve by Sergeant Cecil's subsequent achievements, "but after his first run I told Terry that we had better get this horse handicapped, because all he'll be is a handicapper." Some handicapper.

However, Cooper was a little surprised by the esteem in which the handicapper evidently held the gelding. "He rated him 70 on the turf and 65 on the all-weather, which I thought was a fairly high turf mark for what he'd achieved," he says. Cooper looked more on the ball than the handicapper, certainly at that stage, as Sergeant Cecil's next two runs, one in a maiden and one in a handicap (with Martin Dwyer in the saddle), both at Salisbury over a mile and a half, saw him finish no nearer than mid-division. Cooper was disappointed. "I thought we should have been better than that, considering his run at Bath the previous year," he says. After one of those runs Sergeant Cecil was reluctant to enter the horsebox for the journey back to the yard, prompting Mullins to half-jokingly consider walking him the short distance home instead.

Righton's association with Sergeant Cecil had come to an end after his fourth start. Now a jockeys' agent after a career in the saddle lasting 11 years, he says: "I always thought he was a nice horse, and that he would go on to be a nice horse.

"At that time I hadn't ridden many good horses so I couldn't properly gauge his merit, but looking back on it now he was obviously the best horse I ever rode. I was impressed with him as he progressed - I remember telling Seamus that he had a nice horse who would appreciate a longer trip.

"He was always quite free-going, a keen type, so my main objective was to settle him, to get his head down and teach him to settle in his races. The main thing was to get him to enjoy his job - we worked together on that and it was nice to watch him progress as he did. I liked him, he was a lovely mover, a nice-striding horse.

"When I lost the ride, it was the usual situation I found myself in on many horses - the owners wanted a top jockey and I had to step aside. I'm just glad I had four nice rides on a horse who turned out to be as good as he has. I'm glad the owner let me ride him in the first place."

Sergeant Cecil's next outing, at Sandown, was to prove a watershed in his career. There had long been a school of thought among the stable staff that the further he went, the better he would be. The Sandown race was over a mile and three-quarters, the furthest he had been

asked to go, there were only eight runners, he was right at the bottom of the handicap and was ridden by promising apprentice Fran Ferris. This much was stacked in his favour, despite his 33-1 starting price, and Cooper was expecting a good run.

He ran wide on the first turn, but Ferris managed to settle him in rear until producing him with a threatening challenge two furlongs out. He was still in the first three inside the final furlong, but faded abruptly in the closing stages and was passed by three rivals, ending up sixth, four lengths behind Classic Millennium. Cooper wasn't happy, but Mullins, as ever with Sergeant Cecil, wasn't disappointed.

Mullins says: "At Sandown, Terry fancied him but I didn't. He was adamant the horse had to be ridden handy, but I thought he was better when he was restrained in the early stages. Fran Ferris, who had a much better reputation then than he does now, did nothing wrong and I was quite happy, because I could see we were going places.

"I think it was the straw that broke the camel's back. I came back in smiling and Terry wasn't. But we never fell out over the horse." The plan had been to give Sergeant Cecil a summer break in any case, and Cooper took him back to Paradise. He never returned to Mullins.

Cooper puts his side of the story, saying: "I knew that Seamus was thinking of the horse as a possible jumper, and then when I had him home I just had a feeling that the Sandown race and the Bath

race demonstrated that Cecil had a little bit more in him than we were seeing - it made me think 'this little horse has really got something'. So I decided not to send him back to Seamus, and to send him instead to a Flat yard, where Cecil would have plenty of opportunities to work with horses of his own age and size instead of working with a predominantly jumping string.

"It wasn't Seamus's fault, the way it turned out, it was just how I felt at the time."

There is no animosity now on either side about the decision, although it must have rankled with Mullins at the time that, after all his painstaking 'manufacture' of Sergeant Cecil as a racehorse, another trainer was to reap the benefit of all his hard work.

He says: "It was fair enough - he took the horse for a summer break and never sent it back. I still felt happy that I had done, and was doing, the right thing by the horse. If he had gone to what you might call a 'two-year-old yard', he would probably never have won. If someone had got stuck into him and tried to get results out of him before he was ready, he'd have gone the wrong way mentally.

"Later, Terry was the first to admit I was right - he said to me 'thank God it was you who had him as a young horse and not somebody else'. I'm just delighted to see the horse doing so well now."

Mullins can take solace - although he doesn't appear to need to - in the knowledge that his eminently sensible approach towards Sergeant Cecil moulded the horse correctly at a stage in his life when it would have been very easy for him to go wrong. Mullins and his staff, especially Griffin and Dunford, can count themselves partly responsible for the horse's later phenomenal success,

as in their hands his talent was allowed to develop, whereas in others' it could so easily have been stunted.

Cooper now had another decision to make. After reaching the conclusion that a change was required, he now had to select a new trainer. Where would Sergeant Cecil go next?

# CHAPTER THREE

# THE BEST BIT OF BUSINESS EVER

Never look a gift horse in the mouth. Trainers are completists at heart, eager to fill every box and build more if need be rather than turn a prospective owner away. That was what Cooper was banking on when he embarked upon the search for a new trainer, but what happened left him thinking otherwise.

Of the two names at the top of his list, neither trainer even bothered to get back to him, let alone wander along to take a look at Sergeant Cecil in the flesh. Life is never as simple as it might seem, but for the dubious inconvenience of returning a call and a quick scurry down the road, there are two people out there whose careers might have been very different had they taken the trouble to follow up Cooper's initial request.

He says: "I spoke to David Elsworth and Nerys Dutfield, but neither came to see him, which I thought was a bit strange. He obviously wasn't the greatest prospect in the world, but I was surprised that they didn't even want to come and check him out. David is cursing himself now - Neville saw him at the racecourse and he said 'what a bloody fool I was!'. Mind you, he did have one great stayer in his yard anyway, in Persian Punch, so you can't feel too sorry for him."

Cooper returned to his list and phoned Rod Millman, who had a thriving yard in the village of Kentisbeare, just outside Cullompton, in Devon. Millman was much more amenable to the idea of a new horse and a new owner, and drove up to see Sergeant Cecil a couple of days later. He evidently liked what he saw and, after watching a re-run of his Sandown performance, told Cooper that he thought he'd be able to win a race or two with the gelding. Cooper says: "I suppose plenty of trainers would say the same when trying to bring a new owner into the yard, but he had noticed that Cecil used to 'climb' a bit when he was galloping, he had quite a high knee action, and he thought he could do something about getting him to gallop more fluently, so at least that proved he was thinking about the horse."

The boss – Rod Millman

Sergeant Cecil was on the move again - heading west. Millman says: "I went to Paradise Farm to have a look at one of Neville Poole's horses. Terry was there at the time, showed me Cecil and asked if I'd like to train him. Well, I'd always take a horse if I wasn't full up, but I did have in the back of my mind that nine times out of ten if a horse had been disappointing it meant it was no good.

"I was lucky this time that the horse was just a bit immature - he had been well trained by Seamus, who was only ever guilty of giving the horse time to mature. I was very lucky that I came along and took over a horse who was ready to go on to the next stage of his career." Was it the best bit of business he ever did? "Yes."

Millman had taken charge of a horse he thought he could win with, which was music to the ears of Cooper, who was eager to get off the mark as an owner after years in the wilderness. Music to the ears of Millman, too, who had made a fine fist of a career as a trainer after ploughing an undistinguished furrow as a jump jockey. He had started early, in the Don Hazzard mould, by leaving school at 15 and going to work at Reg Akehurst's yard, where he had earlier cut his teeth with horses during school holidays. "I didn't have any qualifications and I didn't want them," he recalls with a smile. "I was convinced I was going to be a top jockey."

Sooner rather than later he grew too heavy for the Flat, and then went on a tour of west country training establishments including David Barons and Martin Pipe, who had only ten horses during Millman's time at Pond House but managed to supply the hungry jockey with half a dozen winners. Little fish were sweet indeed, as Millman had earlier endured a five-year stretch without riding a winner, which made his persistence and optimism ever more remarkable.

There was the odd shooting star along the way, notably Cobley Express and Tom's Little Al, a popular and talented grey chaser, runner-up in the Mildmay of Flete at Cheltenham and the best Millman ever rode. In all, Millman rode around 40 winners,

The Paddocks, Kentisbeare,
Rod Millman's empire

but 'changed sides' after Gerald Cottrell, for whom he had been riding work, decided to cut back his operation. Millman, backed to the hilt by his wife Louise, rented half Cottrell's yard, 20 boxes, and sent out 12 winners from The Paddocks in his first year, 1990.

The following year he had Royal Seaton, who was good enough to go to Royal Ascot, and after a few years during which his fortunes faded somewhat he popped back up with Lord Kintyre, who landed the valuable Weatherbys Super Sprint at Newbury and thrust the yard back into the limelight. Owners saw that Millman was a good man for two-year-olds, so his yard started filling up with youngsters, nippy and precocious, and his star was soon back in the ascendant. In Sergeant Cecil he had something a little different, a horse who would reward patience, and Millman and his head groom Jim Davies set about settling him in.

"He hadn't done that much hard work before he came to me, but he wasn't the kind of horse you'd want to work too hard, because he was still backward and weak," he says. "He was quite cheeky, a bit of a playboy, more interested in being silly than doing work. He had quite a colty attitude even though he'd been gelded a long time. But we needed to get him on the track, and because there weren't that many races around for a horse of his rating (63), and as he was showing quite a bit of speed at home, I thought I'd drop him down in trip."

Pat Eddery was booked for a mile-and-a-quarter handicap at Chepstow, for which Sergeant Cecil started at 10-1 - better fancied than ever before despite the shorter trip. It was as encouraging an introduction for a new trainer as Millman could have wished for. Eddery managed to settle Sergeant Cecil behind a faster pace than he had experienced in his most recent starts, and they came through inside the final furlong to chase home the winner, Lara Falana, although they never got close enough to throw down a serious challenge.

Everyone was pleased. Work-rider Sharon Steel, who had travelled with him to Chepstow, was taken by the way Sergeant Cecil travelled through the race, although ten minutes earlier he had been travelling in a different direction. She says: "We were in the parade ring while some of the other horses were going down to the start. He wanted to go with them but we weren't ready yet, so all of a sudden he put his head down and started running backwards for a few strides - it certainly gave Pat a shock."

Cooper was delighted. Sergeant Cecil had earned him his very first cheque from Weatherbys - for £1,156 (there was the purchase price back in one fell swoop) - and his expectations of his horse had been justified. It really did look as though his pride and joy had it in him to win a race. Millman kept the ball rolling as Sergeant Cecil kept improving.

Three weeks later he stepped back up in trip and finished third at Beverley, two weeks after that he was runner-up again, this time at Cooper's local track Salisbury, where another valuable lesson was learned. For the first time, Sergeant Cecil found himself in the lead, and as he made his way home from the quarter-mile pole Cooper must have thought his time had come at last. Unfortunately, Sergeant Cecil was in front too long, idled in the closing stages and was worn down on two fronts, flashing past the post almost in unison with Heir To Be and Bobsleigh. Photo-finish.

These days, three horses with no more than a hand's breadth between them can be separated in seconds by computer, but Cooper remembers waiting quite a long time for the result to be called. When the verdict came, Sergeant Cecil was a short head in front of Heir To Be but a neck behind Bobsleigh. He'd drifted across the track, too, ending up on the stands' rail, conceding far more ground than the inches by which he was beaten. The same thing happened at Bath two weeks later, when he made a bold bid for glory a quarter of a mile out before idling in front again, being reeled in and having the spoils snatched away by the fast-finishing Red Wine, who would win the competitive November Handicap at Doncaster on his next start but one. The margin between winning and simply taking part was just a head this time, and the form was solid in a wider context, so for all Cooper's frustration at being constantly denied his first success, there was also hope springing eternal that the elusive win was just around the corner.

It had not gone unnoticed that Sergeant Cecil had failed to sustain an advantage on two occasions. In the early stages of a race he needed to be restrained to prevent his keenness being his undoing; perhaps the brakes should be kept on a little longer, allowing him to delay his decisive move. It was food for thought, Millman also noting that the gelding was a little weak in a finish, something he hoped growth and maturity would mend.

His final outing of the season, his fifth in two months, was at Windsor. Millman was aware that Sergeant Cecil would be off on his winter holidays shortly afterwards and took the opportunity to get another run into him, reasoning that the extra experience would stand him in good stead

Stretching the legs on a crisp spring morning

whatever the outcome. "My job is to win with the horse," he says. "We were running out of time at the end of the season, and he was edging up the handicap with every run without having a victory to show for it. He was improving and I tried to make the most of that."

Wendyll Woods, who went on to become a successful jockey in Hong Kong but on this occasion having his third and final ride on Sergeant Cecil, kept his powder dry until the final quarter-mile, but although the horse ran on gamely he lacked the physical resources to stamp himself on the closing stages of a race and came up short by a length and a half.

That was that; Paradise beckoned and Sergeant Cecil went off to put his feet up through the darkest days of winter, tended hand and foot by his owner, who was learning confidence around horses and the rudiments of stable management from Neville Poole's stock of accumulated wisdom. For Cooper, mucking out was a delight, not a chore, and there were no grumbles at dawn's early light with Sergeant Cecil's white face poking over the box door in greeting.

Cooper was happy with the way things had gone. Four seconds and a third in five races was progress beyond expectation - although never beyond hope! - and the financial rewards, although insignificant, hinted at further remuneration the following season. Racing professionals were even taking note of Sergeant Cecil's progress. "Jason Weaver was commentating on the Windsor race, and he was waxing quite lyrical about Cecil - it was a nice feeling to own a horse who prompted that level of interest," says Cooper.

Millman had done his job well. He hadn't coaxed a win out of Sergeant Cecil, but at that stage of the horse's career such giddy heights were beyond him. He was confident that there was more to come, better to come, and confident in his ability to tap a richer vein from the maturing gelding.

## On the brink

Sergeant Cecil returned to The Paddocks in January and, after putting the fear of God into poor Sharon Steel for a week or two with his freshness and impudence, he settled down to a routine of interval training, steady canters and faster work that gradually honed an edge on his physique. Steel and the other work-riders were required to accommodate his own individual way of getting things done, a carrot generally being the currency he understood best and responded to quickest, but even though those closest to him were biased by their affection towards him, there really was something about him.

Steel recalls: "When he was four, I said he was going to win the Ebor. We were just circling around the yard, either before work or cooling him off afterwards, and he just gave me the impression that he was that type of horse, that winning a big race like the Ebor wouldn't be beyond him." That level of prescience warrants a mighty payout - but did Steel wander down to the local bookies with a handful of readies at the ready? She did not; her reward will have to be found here, proof in black and white of her uncanny ability as a soothsayer. While Steel was predicting the future, Millman was shaping it.

The overwhelming majority of horses in training never win a race; most never finish in the first three. Sergeant Cecil was already slightly ahead of the curve, and a win would make him one of an exclusive minority. All the headlines are about horses winning big races, collecting bankloads of prize-money at home and abroad, being sold for a sheikh's ransom. All the headlines are about a tiny percentage of horses, something that people outside the industry generally fail to grasp. Winning a race is not par for the course; winning a race is your wildest dream come true. Sergeant Cecil was on the brink.

"He came back from holiday a bit bigger and a bit stronger, and was working like a good horse," says Millman. Sergeant Cecil returned to Windsor for his reappearance in a virtually identical race to the one in which he had signed off the previous season. Darryll Holland had the ride, his first experience of the horse, and he opted to play a prominent role. Sent in pursuit of the leader three furlongs from home, Sergeant Cecil showed greater strength under pressure and made the winner, Palamedes, pull out all the stops to prevail by a short head. It was the fifth time he had been second in six starts, and although ostensibly it might look as though he had a bad case of 'seconditis', he wasn't swinging the lead, he wasn't an 'after you, Claude' character, the type rightly regarded by punters as a waste of space.

He hadn't won a race because he hadn't yet been physically or mentally ready to, and it was to his credit, not his demerit, that he had come so close despite these shortcomings. Cooper was thrilled to bits, despite the proximity but ultimate inaccessibility of that longed-for breakthrough. It was a few more quid in the kitty to defray his training expenses and another jolt of excitement to ensure he was happy to pay them.

He had something else to pay, too - the wily Don Hazzard had negotiated that £400 on top of the purchase price should Sergeant Cecil win two races. He had not won anything yet, but after five second-places Cooper reckoned Hazzard was entitled to his money, and wrote him out a cheque as the two left the course.

Millman carefully assessed the evidence, rationalising that

Cecil, Sue & Sharon

56

Sergeant Cecil lacked a turn of foot at this stage of his development and might possibly benefit from the application of blinkers, that aid to concentration occasionally described as a 'rogue's badge' but more often perceived as a welcome slice of assistance to the willing grafter. For his next outing, at Newmarket just over a week later, he decided on a halfway house approach and fitted cheekpieces, sheepskin sideburns that generally lend a horse the raffish air of a Regency rake while encouraging him to keep eyes front. Holland was in the plate for a second time.

"I spoke to Darryll after the Windsor race, and we agreed that he had come a bit too soon on Cecil on that occasion," says Millman. "I then spoke to him the day before and we made a plan to delay Cecil's challenge at Newmarket. The obvious thing to do was not to let him get there too soon this time.

"All my work is done at home, not at the track, you don't train them at the track or at least you're not supposed to, so I didn't go to Newmarket that day, I had work to do in the yard. Most of the time you only go to the races if you have a difficult horse, or if you haven't had a chance to discuss things with a jockey, or (and he smiles) to keep other trainers away from your owners.

"Anyway, I watched the race on television at home, and the first thing I saw was Darryll making the running on him. Cecil ran much too free and ran out of puff. He looked fantastic until they went past him over two furlongs out and he dropped right away after that - it was probably one of his worst runs ever and one we could forget about. Jockeys forget their orders sometimes . . . these things happen."

Cooper, who was at the course, feared the worst after Sergeant Cecil had gone to post "throwing his head around trying to get rid of the cheekpieces", so one way or another the cheekpiece experiment was swiftly abandoned. "I spoke to Rod on the phone, and he said almost exactly the same words as me - 'what a bloody waste of time that was'," says Cooper. Henceforth, Sergeant Cecil has never

Rod and Louise Millman with their happy band of hard workers

worn anything around his head other than a bridle.

Waste of time on the day and waste of time thereafter, too, as Sergeant Cecil had to have a longer break than normal before resurfacing as the Newmarket race had taken plenty out of him, running as he had for more than a mile with the choke out. Three weeks between races is his regular cycle, but it was six weeks before he reappeared at an evening meeting at Sandown over a mile and three-quarters. It was his 14th run. His first win.

## "I was so pleased for the little horse"

"I was thrilled to bits, my first winner after waiting so long," says Cooper. "When you think about my other two horses, and all the seconds Cecil had, to have my first winner was a wonderful feeling, especially at a big track like Sandown. Rod was delighted too.

"My wife Sue and daughter Sam were there, and it was just a wonderful day. We came home with a bronze statuette from the race sponsor, watched the tape of the race and had a glass of champagne or two. I was so pleased for the little horse too, to get a win after all his hard work. I sat back and thought 'we've won now so we'll enjoy it, it might be the last one for a long time - if ever again'. You can't help but think like that."

Millman had drummed into Richard Hughes, who had ridden the horse when he was

60

runner-up to Red Wine at Bath the previous season, the need for restraint in the first half of the race and Hughes, a master of the art of riding a waiting race, brought Sergeant Cecil through to lead just over a furlong out and drove him up the hill to the line, fending off the staying-on Reveillez by a length and a quarter. It was the perfect way to ride the horse, the perfect way to utilise his powers. Reveillez was later bought by JP McManus and has gone on to a rewarding career over hurdles and fences including a Cheltenham Festival victory; the third horse, Manoubi, won on his next outing.

Sergeant Cecil had fulfilled the dreams of Cooper and his family, vindicated Millman's decision to take him on, and justified the hard work required to raise the horse to the level at which he was capable of winning a race. In comparison with the vast majority of his peers he was a success story, and if Millman allowed himself a quiet moment in which to congratulate himself and his staff, or if Cooper uncorked another bottle of champagne and recounted the story thus far once again to his friends and family, then rightly so. No little achievement this - if the horse had never run again, they would always have had Sandown.

However, after the win, Millman described him as no more than "a nice horse", while also according him the status of "one of the better horses in the yard". The handicapper concurred, raising Sergeant Cecil to a mark of 79, the highest of his career. He had come a long way, but there was still a long way to go. Quite how far was anyone's guess.

After his habitual downtime of three weeks, Sergeant Cecil was back at Sandown for an almost identical race, over the same trip and on the same ground, with the presence of Jimmy Fortune in the saddle the only obvious change. In opposition was Sindapour, a year-younger half-brother to Derby winner Sinndar, trained by Martin Pipe for the family of Chanelle Burke, Tony McCoy's wife-to-be, and running over half a mile further than ever before. Additionally, with no insult intended whatsoever to the riders concerned, on Sindapour's two previous starts he had been partnered by lesser lights Robert Cody-Boutcher and Miss Tara Pitman - this time the experienced and talented Martin Dwyer had been booked. Business appeared to be meant and, as it transpired, Sergeant Cecil was attempting the near-impossible in trying to concede Sindapour 12lb.

He ran very well in the circumstances under what we could now call the 'Sergeant Cecil ride'. Fortune moved through from off the pace to challenge just over a furlong out, but the horse began to hang left in the closing stages, and although Fortune evened his keel Sergeant Cecil was to be second again - Sindapour had a comfortable length in hand at the line. On his next outing, just four days later, Sindapour went to Royal Ascot and, in some style, won the two-and-a-half-mile Ascot Handicap from 26 rivals. The penalty he received for the Sandown win was vital in helping him make the cut at Ascot; he had been a 'job' horse and the job was done well. Sergeant Cecil had been entertaining an angel unawares.

There were no such pitfalls in store when, reunited with Hughes and off an official rating of 82, Sergeant Cecil returned to Sandown three weeks later, on the day before the Eclipse Stakes, and ran out a cosy three-quarter-length winner from Mr Ed. He was settled off the pace, brought through to challenge without being asked too many searching questions, and driven out up the hill. Winning by numbers, almost.

Mr Ed went on to be runner-up in the Cesarewitch and also in a valuable Graded event over hurdles at Aintree, while six weeks later fifth-placed Saint Alebe popped up to win the Ebor at 20-1. Sergeant Cecil was keeping the right company - and beating it. The horse had come on in leaps and bounds as a four-year-old, growing into his frame all the time and matching that physical development with increasing mental strength and resolution. Hughes told Cooper in the aftermath that "two furlongs out your horse was hard on the bridle", underlining his amenability to restraint and the potent force available when he was husbanded thus. Millman had fathomed his tactical requirements and everyone was reaping the benefit.

The only worm in the apple was the fact that this win had sent Sergeant Cecil's handicap mark up to a peak of 87, meaning that he was ineligible for 0-85 handicaps and therefore obliged to take on stronger opposition.

"We were delighted that he'd won the race, but the first impression afterwards was that it was going to be harder now because the handicapper would raise him out of 0-85 company," says Millman. "But you can't complain, you've got an improving horse, one who is doing better all the time, and you have to take the consequences." In a bid to ride the wave, Millman sent Sergeant Cecil to Ascot eight days later for a £37,000 handicap, very much a step into the big league and also a step up in distance to two miles. "A little bit of a disaster," remembers Cooper. "For some reason he made the running that day and, as he was a hold-up horse really, it was never going to work out. I don't think Richard (Hughes) had too much choice in the matter, as he was drawn wide and Cecil is usually smartly away, and being a two-mile race there wouldn't have been much early pace to help him cover up the horse.

"Cecil loves passing horses – I reckon it gives him a bit of a buzz each time he goes past one – and if he's in front too long he gets bored."

Hughes knew that a forcing ride was not suitable for Sergeant Cecil, and so he reluctantly set no more than a moderate gallop in a bid to settle him in front over a trip that was an unknown quantity. It didn't work; Sergeant Cecil pulled Hughes's arms out in front and was a spent force fully two furlongs out, eventually finishing eighth, a place behind stablemate Zibeline, having his last run for Millman after twice finishing third in the Northumberland Plate and fifth in the Ebor. If there was a sense of the baton being passed, no-one was setting too much store by it at this stage. Indeed, Millman had let his thoughts wander down a different path. "His form had got better and better, but when his handicap mark hit 87 I thought about sending him hurdling," he says. He doesn't say how long he thought about it, but one suspects it wasn't for very long.

However, he wasn't the only one who could picture Sergeant Cecil stretching his legs over hurdles, as it was at about that time that Millman was made aware of a big offer for the gelding to go jumping. He says: "Terry was offered £150,000-plus for Cecil, and was very pleased and quite proud to find he had a horse worth that sort of money, but no way would he sell." Sell the horse named as a memorial to his father? Fat chance.

Sergeant Cecil needed a longer rest after his bout of fruitless front-running, and it was a month before his next outing in one of the Shergar Cup races back at Ascot. The Shergar Cup, a six-race international jockeys' challenge, has not wholly captured the imagination but at least provides an opportunity to watch top jockeys from around the world in action at close quarters. The riding arrangements are determined by lot, and Sergeant Cecil got lucky when Kieren Fallon's name came out of the hat alongside his. That was where the good luck dried up.

The gelding, who raced keenly as usual but was anchored in rear by a forewarned Fallon, made progress a quarter of a mile out and went to wriggle his way through a gap to challenge at the furlong pole, but he was in effect sandbagged from both sides as the gap closed. Fallon dragged him out to renew his challenge, but the post came too soon and Capitano Corelli, ridden by Australian jockey Shane Dye, held on by three-quarters of a length, which was a bit of a teeth-grinder because it was Dye's mount who had been mostly to blame for the interference.

"He was completely blocked off half a furlong out," says Cooper. "Kieren had to rein back and pull him round, and if the race had been 100 yards or so longer we'd have got up. Kieren was fuming when he came back in and told the stewards that it definitely cost him the race. The stewards had a look but left the placings unaltered - we were all very disappointed, and it was fortunate that Cecil didn't get struck into.

"He was like a terrier, though, he didn't down tools when he was messed around with but stuck out his head and charged up the rails, only just too late."

Next time out, at Haydock in the Old Borough Cup, it was another bad day, a write-off. Millman and Cooper had reservations about the firm going at the Lancashire track, but a prolonged downpour in the hours before the race eased their worries as

well as the ground. However, heavy rain on fast ground brings its own problems, as only the top three or four inches become saturated and are therefore easily removed, leaving very fast ground underneath. Richard Hughes was back in the saddle, and the legacy of his previous ride at Ascot, when

Sergeant Cecil ended up making the running, led to an unfortunate scenario.

Millman says: "Because he ran off with Richard the previous time he rode him, this time Hughesy did the conventional thing and missed the break, sitting back in last place. However, the other 18 runners were kicking off the top of the turf and it was all coming back and hitting him in the face.

"Well, he didn't want to know then, and he ran a terrible race. Hughesy is a great jockey for a tactical ride on a horse who's cruising along, but he isn't the most muscular jockey, not the greatest of enforcers, and it would have taken an extremely strong ride to change Cecil's mind about that race. They got further and further behind and trailed home with only two behind them. We decided to stop for the season after that."

"We'd had a thrilling year," says Cooper. "We'd had two wins and three seconds, and we thought that it had all been well worth waiting for. To do what we did with him that season was the thrill of a lifetime for a small owner like me."

CHAPTER FOUR

# THAT'S IT–
# I'M RETIRING HIM

The routine was well established, and Sergeant Cecil loves his routine. As usual, he spent two or three months at Paradise Farm Stud before returning to Millman's yard in January to begin preparation for the new season. Every horse in the yard has its work tailored to its ongoing needs, as is the case in training establishments the world over, but Sergeant Cecil's very individual habits give Millman and his staff plenty to think about.

Jumps trainer Philip Hobbs attempted to demystify the art of training racehorses by saying "there's an awful lot of bullshit talked about training horses. It's just twice up the gallops every day and run them when you want", which is an admirably grounded perspective but one that fails to encompass the intricacies of raising Sergeant Cecil to peak fitness.

Millman explains: "When he comes back to us, he's on the gallop within a week. He walks and trots for the first few days, around the trotting ring and not on the local roads because he's too silly, and then he's ready to go up the gallops.

"During the first ten days he'll be trying to buck Sharon off whenever he can. He always goes out first lot behind a lead horse, because he's a hold-up horse even on the gallops. Sharon rides him and her partner Sean is usually on the lead horse, although obviously it's not always the same horse, and these days we wouldn't have that many in the yard quick enough to work with him.

"Of course, we try to get him as fit as we can, but whatever we do he invariably needs his first run of the season. Cecil goes on the gallop more often and does more work than any other horse I've had, but he still always needs a run - or even two - to be 100 per cent.

"I do interval training here because I only have a short gallop, so when I need to give him a stiffer test I take him up the road to Stuart Kittow's yard - but Cecil has got wise to that now and he doesn't like it, because it makes him work too hard.

Cecil's groom Sue Davey with her pride and joy

He's an enthusiastic worker at home because he doesn't find it too hard - but after the first trip or two up Stuart's gallop he loses interest. It gives him a bit of an extra blowout anyway."

Sharon Steel knows all about his enthusiasm on home soil, being the one at the sharp end of the exuberant chestnut's work detail. She laughs as she explains, but it's easy to imagine that on some mornings it's not a laughing matter. "He's hard to pull up at the top of the gallop, because he's usually tanking along at that stage as he simply must pass his lead horse before he stops. He loves to 'win' his gallop," she says.

"He settles in behind his lead, but whoever's leading us has to pull up on the right-hand side near the end of the run and leave me room to go past, so that he'll stop when he finds himself in front, otherwise he'd just keep going.

"I have to work with him, have to accommodate his funny ways. I have to let him go just so far, and then draw the line. If you try to boss him along he doesn't like it, and as he gets fitter and feels better he does it all himself. He starts taking himself along and then I find I've got a job to pull him up."

Seamus Mullins had discovered that Sergeant Cecil had his own ideas about everything, and age certainly hadn't affected his thought processes. He liked to do things in his own way at his own pace, and to try to impose a different discipline was to court failure. Sooner or later, everyone found that out.

Now fit again, or as fit as he would ever be first time, hopes were high that he would come out as a five-year-old and continue his progress up the handicap towards more prestigious and more valuable races, but everyone had to take a step back after his reappearance. He went to Epsom for the Great Metropolitan Handicap, a great race in its Victorian heyday but no more than a notable handicap now, on ground officially described as soft. As had happened at Haydock on his last start the previous season, he had mud kicked in his face and, in common with the traditional seven-stone weakling, he didn't like it. Richard Hughes didn't persevere with him when it was obvious that he was hating every minute and he finished a distant last of 20.

Now, Terry Cooper lives and breathes Sergeant Cecil, and occasionally takes the slings and arrows of outrageous fortune to heart where his pride and joy is concerned. When left to calm down for a couple of hours he's as right as ninepence, but his propensity for temporary Sergeant Cecil-based tunnel vision let him down on this occasion.

"Terry wanted to retire him!" laughs Millman. "He didn't take the race very well at all, so I told him that there was only room for one bad loser in the yard and that was me."

"He didn't fire at all that day," says Cooper, "and I was worrying that we'd lost him, that his last run the previous season and his first run that season meant that he'd peaked and was on the way down. I probably over-reacted, but all I was worrying about was that the horse was letting himself down, and I wasn't going to have that."

Millman, who has by now stopped laughing, adds: "I had Cecil scoped, and there was a little bit of muck in his throat but not enough to make him run as badly as that. However, our vet had a look at him and it turned out that he had a little problem with his sinuses, so we gave him some antibiotics to clear it up. It's the only time he's ever run with a bit of sickness on him."

Cooper wasn't the only one with misgivings. Steel thought he'd 'gone' too, but Millman rode him in a couple of gallops and reckoned otherwise. The show would go on, although the Epsom race was an unfortunate end to Hughes's association with the horse. Hughes had partnered him to his first two victories, forging the breakthrough that later led to fame and fortune. He says: "He was quite a free runner, so the job was always to settle him early on. He was a good little horse, always honest, but I never thought he'd improve so much and get to where he is now."

Sergeant Cecil had had what was for him a long break - almost two months - before he returned to action at Goodwood under 10st, when Millman was keen to reverse the recent trend of his getting behind in races while taking into account the fact that he didn't want to be too involved too early. The handicapper had shown him a little leniency, dropping him 4lb for his two lacklustre outings, but the Great British Punter was surely going too far by letting him start at 33-1. Steve Drowne, having his first ride on the horse, was charged with treading the fine line between too far back and too forward and carried it off well, putting the horse into the race three furlongs out and taking it up a furlong later, before - the old story from his three-year-old days - Sergeant Cecil failed to find a great deal in front and was passed by two horses inside the final furlong, finishing a two-length third behind Wait For The Will. He seemed back on the right road, his mind on winning races again after two very forgettable displays.

Well, not quite. Next time out at Sandown, in the race he had won the previous year, his headstrong nature proved too much even for the iron will of Kieren Fallon, who couldn't restrain him as he pulled for his head just behind the leaders. He ran himself to a standstill, showing a touch of temperament and finishing a long way behind Quedex. Cooper says: "When he came back up the rhododendron walk at Sandown, he was jig-jogging along and looked as fresh as he had before he went to post. He wasn't blowing at all."

Millman says: "That group of four races was the worst run he had ever put together, and the worst he ever would put together. There were reasons for those poor shows, but it was a disappointing time. Terry and I felt he had barely had a race at Sandown, given the way he ran, so I sent him out again quickly at Ascot a week later."

It was like the sun coming out after the rain. Reunited with Jimmy Fortune, who had been aboard in Sindapour's race at Sandown, and given the 'Sergeant Cecil ride', he came swooping through from last place to lead a furlong out and was driven home to inch out Cutting Crew, who went on to win a valuable handicap at Glorious Goodwood on his next start, by a short head, the photo-finish going in his favour for once.

"To win at Ascot was something special," says Cooper. "The race was worth about £10,000, so it wasn't exactly the most valuable contest ever run there, but at that stage of his career it was pretty big for us. Neville Poole was with me that day, and before Cecil's race he picked a piece of heather from the display at the front of the royal box and gave it to me, saying 'here you are, here's some good luck'. I popped it in my jacket pocket and Neville went off to have a bet, and he came back and said that Cecil was 22-1.

"Now, I'm not a betting man, although Sue likes her Saturday gamble, but I thought that was a bit of an insult and I had a tenner each-way at 20-1 - I haven't backed him since. Neville and I

Head down and driving hard –
Sergeant Cecil and Jimmy Fortune
(left) in winning style at Ascot

were watching the race together and from where we were it looked very close, I wasn't sure whether he had won. Neville was sure, he said 'trust me, I know about these things, we've won', and he put his arm round me and dragged me off to the winner's enclosure.

"Obviously, that was before they rebuilt Ascot, and to see Cecil walking through the old gates into the no.1 spot at Ascot, like so many great champions before him, was an incredible feeling. You could say the heather worked!"

With the bandwagon rolling once again, Sergeant Cecil was entered in a valuable handicap at Glorious Goodwood almost three weeks later. The chestnut runs regularly, more often than the very top echelon, and this is for two reasons. First, there are generally sufficient races in which to run him, granted his rating and requirements, in comparison to horses who flit like butterflies from Group 1 to Group 1, often waiting three months for their next assignment, and second, because it appears to suit his metabolism. Millman says: "He's at his best when running every three weeks. It's much harder to train him to run every six weeks than it is to run every three weeks, because I

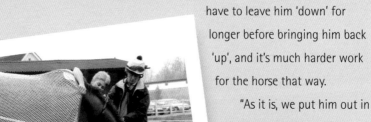

have to leave him 'down' for longer before bringing him back 'up', and it's much harder work for the horse that way.

"As it is, we put him out in a paddock for a couple of days after a race, because he's quite dull for a couple of days afterwards, exhausted by his exertions, and then put him back in work and start building him up again. He hasn't got quite so far to bounce back from if we try to keep to a three-week cycle."

Millman had the Ebor at York at the back of his mind for Sergeant Cecil, but the gelding was too far down the weights to be certain of making the cut-off point. A win at Goodwood would bring with it a 7lb penalty, which would push him up the pecking order and increase his chance of taking part. Fortune had the ride again and attempted a carbon-copy of his Ascot tactics, but what suits one race doesn't always suit another and, although Fortune settled him in the early stages and brought him through to lead over a furlong out, the effort involved in finessing through the hectic Goodwood traffic - a notorious course for hard-luck stories - possibly proved his downfall, as he had nothing more to give when Mephisto flashed past in the last 100 yards.

It was Mephisto, not Sergeant Cecil, who went on to Ebor glory in his next race, but the horse had still done everyone proud by producing what the *Racing Post* race analyst called "the race of his life, for he has never won off a mark this high (89)". Cooper's regular comment when things have gone well is "thrilled to bits", and that phrase got another airing. Millman hadn't been so thrilled before the race, as Sergeant Cecil was reluctant to climb into his horsebox to make the journey from the racecourse stables to the track, and the trainer had to get a lift down the hill to the stables to change the wilful gelding's mind with the bristly end of a broom.

## "I just felt he needed a bit of luck"

Sergeant Cecil had moved into a different league now. His days of mixing it in £10,000 contests were over; he had shown at Goodwood that he belonged in the best and most competitive handicaps, a scenario well beyond the expectations of Cooper on the day he paid Don Hazzard £1,000 for the little chestnut. And not only could Cooper daydream about his horse and how much further the trail might lead, he could also begin to read about him in the papers. Before his next outing, another tilt at Haydock's Old Borough Cup, the daily tipping section in the *Racing Post* featured, below the headline 'Sergeant looks the one to beat following latest clockbuster', the advice of Topspeed guru Dave Edwards, who may have been one of the first of many (so many) to resort to a military slant when writing: "Sergeant Cecil has earned his stripes in strongly run races and can assert his authority in the Stanleybet.com Old Borough Heritage Handicap (2.05) at Haydock. The Rod Millman-trained five-year-old won narrowly at Ascot in July, and posted a personal best on the clock later in the month at Goodwood when beating all bar subsequent Ebor winner Mephisto in the fastest race on the card."

The ground was more suitable at Haydock, but the race was a more competitive affair and the handicapper had elevated Sergeant Cecil to a mark of 93, his highest yet. Drowne was back in the saddle and did his best to anchor the perpetually keen type, although Millman later felt that the horse was still running too freely for his own good. He says: "He ran a good race but he didn't relax as well as he can, and I thought he should have been held up a bit more, I thought he was a bit too close to the action.

"Having said that, Steve rode a good race, he did nothing wrong, and was only beaten three-quarters of a length into second place. I felt at the time that the performance was as good as the horse was, that he had run right up to the peak of his ability."

Drowne says: "That day we just bumped into a very well-handicapped horse of James Fanshawe's, but I remember that for a horse who stayed long distances Cecil had a very good turn of foot, plenty of pace."

Second place behind Defining earned Cooper £16,000, by some way the biggest payout of his career as an owner, and considering the winner went on to be third in a Yorkshire Cup and the third horse Sendintank had won eight of his previous nine races, he had ample reason to be thankful that he hadn't retired the horse after his first run of the season. It would have been a mistake, wouldn't it, Terry?

The previous year Sergeant Cecil had been roughed off after Haydock, but the boot was on the other foot this time and there were still arses to be kicked. Millman decided upon a swift turnaround and six days later sent Sergeant Cecil to Doncaster for the Mallard Handicap, a similar race in many respects to the Old Borough Cup but with half the prize-money. The game of musical jockeys proceeded, with Drowne giving way to Fortune, who kept up his record of never finishing out of the first two on Sergeant Cecil.

The well-backed and lightly weighted Lost Soldier Three, ridden prominently, got first run on Sergeant Cecil and maintained the advantage all the way to the line although the chestnut plugged on in game style, going under by a length and a quarter. Millman was happy with everything bar the result, as Fortune had stuck to the 'Sergeant Cecil ride' gameplan and only circumstance had thwarted him. He says: "He ran a blinder, coming from way off the pace, but because he started from so far back he couldn't get through the traffic, and consequently couldn't get there in time. In these big-field handicaps you've got a lot of horses to come through, and if the gaps don't open at the right time you're in trouble."

Millman felt there was more in the tank, doing his job of maximising the horse's chances of winning a race. Sergeant Cecil had not had a hard season and his hardy constitution could cope with another trip to the well. After three second places over a mile and three-quarters, Millman dropped him back to a mile and a half at Ascot where,

Sergeant Cecil and Jimmy Fortune (left) gallant in defeat behind Lost Soldier Three (centre) at Doncaster

with Fortune booked, the *Racing Post*'s race trends expert Craig Thake considered it might be his day, writing "perennial big-handicap bridesmaid Sergeant Cecil is taken to go one better for Rod Millman, who was a short head away from winning this in 1994".

Fortune settled him at the rear of the field in a virtual repeat of his Doncaster exploits, but this time two horses slipped the field a long way out and Sergeant Cecil could never land a glove on them. Third was the best he could manage, a bridesmaid again as the improving three-year-old Fort, himself third to Sergeant Cecil at Ascot in July, enjoyed his big day. Fortune says: "I remember the first day I rode him - he was a headstrong horse and quite hard to settle. He wasn't straightforward, he took a bit of knowing. I always felt he had plenty of ability, but when I rode him he wasn't half the horse he turned out to be."

It could have been called an unsatisfactory end to the season, as after victory at Ascot the horse had narrowly missed landing a valuable handicap on four occasions, an echo of his three-year-old career when there always seemed to be one too good on the day, but, as Cooper says, that would have been missing the point. "We collected third-place prize-money and had another good day out at a big track, so complaining about not winning seems rather picky. We kept going

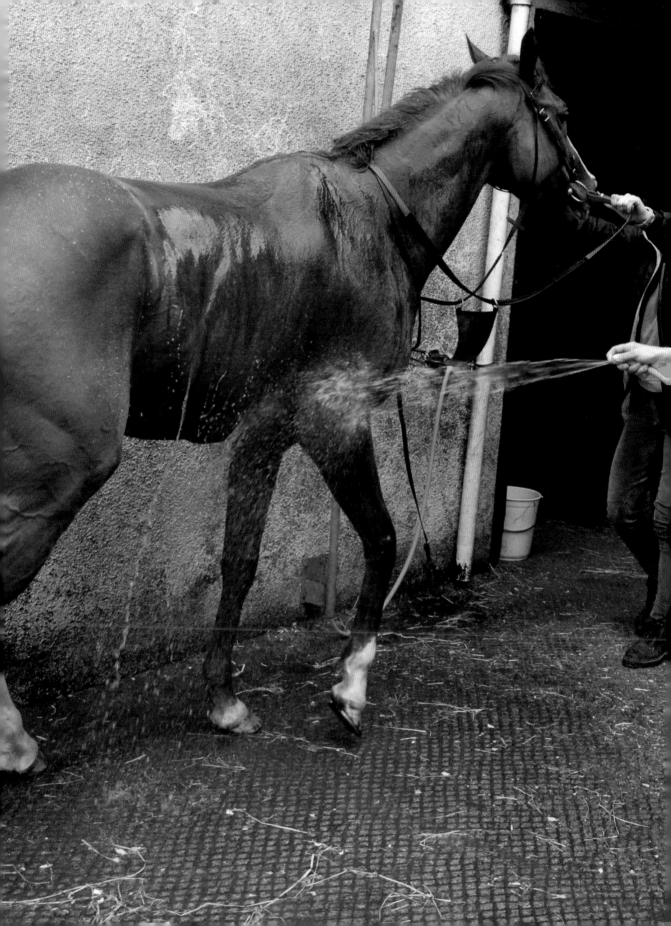

racing and nearly every time we were placed, and that spoils you a little bit.

"We'd had another good season, another successful year, and we'd never dreamt that we'd have a horse who would do what he'd done. He'd moved up to another level, and so even though he wasn't winning we were still thrilled to bits."

That phrase again - and the thrills went hand in hand with not having to pay the bills, as Cooper calculated that only once since Millman had taken over the horse had he been required to send Weatherbys a cheque for entries, colours renewal, administrative fees, etc. Happiness is . . . equine self-sufficiency.

There wasn't much left in the programme book for Sergeant Cecil as October dawned, but as Poole prepared a box for the returning warrior, Millman confessed to the odd nag of frustration. "I thought he was running as well as he could and to a level that was as good as he was ever going to be, but I just felt he needed a bit of luck," he says. "We were running consistently off a mark of 93, but we were conceding too much ground through being held up in big fields."

Beneath the public veil of the connections' satisfaction, there was the impression of a yearning for something a little bit better again. They were thankful for what they had received, but Lord, wouldn't they have just loved something to make them truly thankful. Cooper had given voice to this desire a couple of times during the season, buttonholing Millman with the words "I just want to win one big one, just one big race".

And that's the great thing about racing - you never know.

CHAPTER FIVE

# ALAN WHO?

At the start of his six-year-old season, Sergeant Cecil had run 27 times, been ridden by ten different jockeys, won three races, been placed in 13 more, and earned £85,610.50 in win and place prize-money. By any standard, he was an unqualified success, especially considering he cost his owner Terry Cooper a grand total of £1,400 and had failed to win a race until the summer of his four-year-old campaign.

He had come a long way in a relatively short time, but there was now the question of whether he had it in him to go further, or whether he had already fulfilled every shred of his ability and potential and was destined now to tread over old ground before starting an inevitable and irreversible decline. At that moment, hopes were high, fuelled by the success of the previous 18 months, but everyone involved with the horse knew that their fortunes could change in an instant.

Millman decided to take him to Epsom again for his reappearance and again chose the Great Met, not placing too much importance on the outcome of the race because Sergeant Cecil was sure to need the run and to benefit considerably from it. Cooper wasn't altogether delighted by another trip to Epsom, as he believed Sergeant Cecil was unsuited by the track's undulations and the fierce camber up the home straight, but he also reasoned that the first race was a shot to nothing. It would also be a good opportunity for his new rider to get a feel of the horse without being burdened by too much pressure.

Alan Munro was a familiar name to British racegoers - those with a decent memory. Those who had seen him partner the mighty Generous to victory in the Derby, Irish Derby and King George in 1991 are unable to forget him, but those whose interests in the sport blossomed after the mid-1990s can be forgiven for asking "Alan who?"

Munro rode his first winner in 1985, and honed his talents over the next few years with northern trainer Mel Brittain and by frequent visits to America, where he developed the streamlined crouch style of riding that made him instantly recognisable among his more conventional peers. In 1990 he forged a partnership with Newmarket trainer Bill O'Gorman, who helped him increase his prominence and standing with rides on the likes of prolific two-year-old Timeless Times and Royal Ascot winner Mac's Imp.

Better was to come the following season when, out of the blue, he was offered a three-year contract to ride Fahd Salman's powerful band of horses, including Generous, and grabbed his big chance with both hands. The good times continued to roll, but his contract wasn't renewed and, after a year's unsatisfactory freelancing, he left Britain to ride in Japan and Hong Kong.

In an interview in the *Racing Post* as he prepared for his British comeback, he told Mark Blackman: "Hong Kong's a fantastic place. I was there for ten years, and it became home. But by June 2000, I'd just burnt out. To ride races you need to want to do it, it needs to be a passion, and at that time it had just kind of run out for me.

"I'd wanted to do martial arts since I was about five, but you can't do it seriously when you're racing. I also knew it would keep me in good shape for returning to racing. Had I not done martial arts, my condition now would have been terrible as, basically, I never saw a horse for four and a half years."

Alan Munro punches the air after winning the 1991 Derby on Generous

After riding with success in Hong Kong for nine years, Munro decided to take a complete break from race-riding in the wake of one of his biggest wins, on Industrialist in the Queen Elizabeth II Cup at Sha Tin in April 2000. He spent his sabbatical honing his karate skills, rising to the rank of black belt and keeping mind and body fit and free from the pressures of the day-to-day grind. Four years later, he reached the stage where he wanted to give racing another chance.

In the same interview, he admitted: "Racing has been a good outlet for me - if you take me out of racing there's not much that I fit into. You step out into the real world for five years, and nothing comes with you when you leave racing. No-one calls and you lose your identity - you have to readjust to being just a small person in the world and it's really hard. I'm sure I'll get the opportunities, so if I don't establish myself again it'll be because I messed up."

Millman knew Munro's British agent, Jonathan Ramsden, and thought he'd try him out. "I said we'd get him down here for a look, and maybe we'd have a few horses for him to ride in races. I thought at worst he'd be able to ride work," he says.

"I went to pick him up at the station, and this small figure came shambling up the platform, wearing badly scuffed trainers, with his jeans all worn down at the back, and the first thing he said was 'cor Rod, you've aged!'.

"He'd been riding in New Zealand, where I think he'd had a couple of wins, but it was summer over there and it was winter over here, and he wasn't really prepared for the cold mornings. We kitted him out and looked after him a bit, and I sent him up the gallops. When I came back after first lot, the first thing I said to Louise was 'he's still got it, he'll be all right'.

"He hadn't ridden for five years and I doubt he'd watched much racing in that time, horses aren't his life like they are for some riders, but he's a jockey through and through and he's intelligent, he's a deep thinker."

Millman had been impressed by Munro, and Cooper also warmed to the jockey. He says: "I got on with Alan from day one. One nice thing I found out about him immediately was that when you spoke to him, he listened. He even listened to me, someone who knew next to nothing about horses. I can tell you, not all jockeys do that."

The Millman-Munro axis enjoyed a dream start. Millman had a phalanx of cheap two-year-olds who were bred to be fast and trained to be ready. Munro was ready to go, too, and rode Millman's first eight winners of the season, during which hot streak he rode Sergeant Cecil for the first time. Munro had been apprised of the constituents of the 'Sergeant Cecil ride', and considered that the chances of getting it right regularly were slim to say the least, given the varied factors that had to fall into place.

At Epsom, it didn't go right, although nobody really expected it to. Sergeant Cecil needed the race and Munro gave him an easy time when it was obvious that little was to be gained by giving him a hard time. "He wasn't fully fit and the ground was slow," he says, "and given those conditions a horse just stops when it gets a bit tired." Sergeant Cecil trailed in twelfth of 13 behind Tender Falcon, a short-lived effort having petered out early in the straight. Cooper took it on the chin; there were no calls for the horse's retirement.

Just over three weeks later, the going was totally different at Newbury, very fast ground, and Sergeant Cecil, with a run under his belt, was much more like his usual self. Munro settled him at the back of

Generous wins the 1991 King George

the field and brought him snaking through on the rail three furlongs out, only to find his way barred by Highland Games and Kieren Fallon. "I shouted for Kieren to give me some room, and then he really flew home, but the winner was out of reach," says Munro. "I was impressed, though, he showed a lot of potential when he had room to race." Flamboyant Lad beat him by three lengths - second again.

With Munro and Sergeant Cecil acclimatising nicely to each other, three weeks later Millman sent him back to Epsom for a valuable mile-and-a-half handicap on Derby day. Munro had finished runner-up in the big race on Walk In The Park earlier in the afternoon, and continued the process of getting to the bottom of the chestnut gelding in the last race on the card.

"This was an interesting race," he says. "Every race on Sergeant Cecil was like a voyage of discovery. The basics were there, but there were a lot of variables to take into account. He wasn't completely set in his ways tactically - he needed to be switched off, but even if he was switched off in the early stages he could still get lit up during the race. He's better

Sergeant Cecil and Alan Munro pip It's The Limit for second place behind Flamboyant Lad at Newbury

covered up, but he doesn't actually need to be covered up.

"One day you could ride him without cover, because it so happened that you couldn't cover him up, and he'd run as well as he ever had. Equally, you could come down the outside, without any cover, and he would run flat. He's a very hard horse to say what works best with him, but you can say he is better with cover. And he got fitter, which helped, but the great thing about him was that he also began to develop some track-craft, a race pattern. I think he came of age, he completed the maturing process, which was a big help to me. Instead of leaving the stalls with the priority being to settle him, I could break with the priority being to get a good position, because I knew that he wouldn't be too keen. It gave me a lot of confidence."

Which, in turn, Munro instilled back into the horse. They were becoming a team.

Another new member of Team Cecil was Sue Davey, who had taken over as Sergeant Cecil's groom towards the end of the previous season, aided and abetted in the acquisition of her new best friend by her old friend Sharon Steel. The pair gelled very satisfactorily, Davey adapting to Sergeant Cecil's various little habits and providing him with a comforting presence in the mornings and at the racecourse. However, she got more than she bargained for at Epsom.

"We were walking around the parade ring before the race, and I think he must have caught sight of something out of the corner of his eye, maybe on the big screen they have there," she says.

"Anyway, he whipped his head round and caught me across the face. He knocked me out. The next thing I remember was lying on the ground looking up at him looking down at me. He looked quite surprised, but not as surprised I was. It hurt a lot, but there was no lasting damage - and the following day he bought me a bunch of flowers to say sorry." He was lucky Millman hadn't stopped his pocket-money.

Sergeant Cecil was drawn on the wide outside at Epsom, but as the field drifted over to the far rail after leaving the stalls Munro was able to drop him into mid-division, from where he began a run down the outside three furlongs out. With a furlong and a half to run he was second, zeroing in on the leader Crow Wood, but he flattened out inside the final furlong and was passed by Balkan Knight, eventually going under by two and a half lengths. It was another step up the ladder.

Millman says: "This was the first time I realised we had a better horse. I thought he had the race won all the way down the straight, but then he idled and switched off inside the final furlong. I could see why he didn't win, there was an obvious reason, and I was really pleased with him."

It was time to grasp the nettle. The previous year, Sergeant Cecil had been an Ebor candidate but failed to make the cut for the big York handicap. This season, slightly higher in the handicap and apparently a good deal more mature and malleable, the Ebor was again the major target. But before the Ebor came the Northumberland Plate at Newcastle - exactly three weeks after his Epsom run - and that's where he went next.

## "I just want to win one big one"

"It was a dream come true." "It was a fuck-up." "It was too far to go, so I stayed at home." Try to match the comments to one of Sergeant Cecil's connections . . .

The Northumberland Plate forms part of the backbone of British racing. First run in 1833, it is one of the enduring landmarks of the Flat season, defeating the passage of time and the vagaries of fashion to retain its relevance in an age several worlds removed from the one in which it was conceived more than 170 years ago. The two-mile handicap was known during its heyday as the Pitmen's Derby, as every miner worth his salt for miles around used to descend on the racecourse with his family for an afternoon's sport. These days its nickname is still widely used, even though the only pitmen known to 21st-century racefans are Jenny, Richard and Mark.

Sergeant Cecil was stepping back up in distance for the Plate, having not tried the marathon trip since the unfortunate day at Ascot almost two years earlier when he had made the running. Millman had saddled Zibeline to be placed twice in the race and was confident that Sergeant Cecil would stay, and so was Tom Segal, Pricewise of the *Racing Post*, whose hugely influential tipping column came down heavily on his side.

Under the headline '20-1 Sergeant Cecil set to dispel any stamina doubts', the master tipster wrote: "Provided the ground stays on the quick side at Newcastle for the Northumberland Plate, it could be worth chancing the stamina of Sergeant Cecil at a huge price. This is a top-quality handicapper who looked to be running into peak form when 'looping' the whole field turning for home in a hot handicap at Epsom last time before finishing third.

"The form was given a boost when the winner Crow Wood nearly won at Royal Ascot at York last week, and Sergeant Cecil never runs a bad race when the ground is on the lively side. The trip is a slight worry, but in some of the best mile-and-three-quarter handicaps last year he was staying on best of all late on, and it could be that the step up to two miles sees him improve on what is already rock-solid form.

"This race often goes to the horse who challenges last of all and from stall seven he looks to be nicely positioned, and in Alan Munro he has one of the better tactical jockeys around. If the ground is quick - and we often over-exaggerate the likely ground transition if there is rain about - he is certainly no 20-1 shot."

Craig Thake also tipped him, in his Ten-Year Trends column, and it seemed as though here, finally, was a chance for Cooper to win his 'big one'. However, while Segal and Thake were filing their encouraging copy, Cooper himself was wondering whether the whole thing was worth the candle.

"Cecil went to Newcastle the day before the race, and I travelled up that morning too," he says. "It was pouring with rain when I left Blandford, and I'd got as far as Oxford before everything came to a halt. A lorry had broken down and the traffic was all over the place - it took about an hour and a quarter to drive what you would normally do in ten minutes. On top of that, the rain was coming down so hard I could barely see a thing.

"I thought to myself 'is it worth going all the way to Newcastle, or shall I turn round now and go home?' Then I told myself that Cecil had to travel up there through all these problems, so the least I could do was go up there as well.

"It was just one of those days, the M1 was solid too. It got to six o'clock and I was still on the M1, so I stopped at the services to find a bed for the night and start with a clean slate the following morning. I didn't sleep, though, I never do the night before - I was tense about the journey and tense about the race."

Cooper resumed his journey early the following morning, but on arrival at Newcastle was disappointed to find that the rain had hit the track overnight. With

Sergeant Cecil ensconced in his box, Cooper, Davey and travelling head groom Jack Micklem walked the course, fearing to find a mudbath fit to end any slim hopes they had of victory. They were pleasantly surprised. "The sun was peering through and there was a nice breeze helping to dry the track, and there were no puddles on the course itself," says Cooper. "We decided to be a bit scientific and worked out where the going was best. Down the back straight we needed to be within six feet of the rail, and in the home straight we either wanted to be tight to the rail or four or five metres off it."

Millman had stayed behind in Devon – "It was too far to go, and I had work to do at home" – and Cooper was on his own at Newcastle. His wife Sue, a regular fixture when Sergeant Cecil did battle on the racecourses of Britain, unfortunately had to be elsewhere.

"Poor old Sue, she had recently been diagnosed with breast cancer," says Cooper. "It was at about that time that she was having chemotherapy, so when I found myself a quiet corner, I said a little prayer for her. It helped to calm me down - Sue Davey said I was looking as relaxed as she'd ever seen me at the races, and for some reason I just had the feeling that father and the good Lord were looking down on me. I wasn't expecting Cecil to win, just to run a good race, and that took some of the pressure off too."

As Cooper was on his own, he had a couple of spare badges, so in a bid to spread a little happiness, he went in search of suitable recipients. "Some people think you're a spiv when you wander up and ask them if they'd like tickets," he says, looking not in the least bit spiv-like. "They tell you to push off. Anyway, I went up to one young lad and offered him the badges. He was a marine and had a couple of mates on their way to the track, so I handed them over and told him to make sure they behaved themselves, as my name was on the badges."

Sergeant Cecil was one of a maximum field of 20 for the John Smith's-sponsored contest, the interest sparked by Segal's recommendation driving his price down to 14-1. Even Sir Clement Freud had backed him, and wrote about it in his next *Racing Post* column. There were several familiar faces in the field - last year's Epsom winner Cold Turkey, Haydock third Sendintank, recent Epsom runner-up Balkan Knight, High

Action and Pagan Dance - but the hot favourite was recent Royal Ascot at York fifth Swift Sailor, from Mark Johnston's yard. It was a tough, tight, keenly contested field, and Sergeant Cecil had just scraped into it on the joint-lowest rating of 92. He was fit and fancied. Was this the big one Cooper had coveted for so long?

It didn't look that way when the stalls opened. Sergeant Cecil was in front. Munro says: "The Northumberland Plate was a mess. It was what you call a fuck-up. I was confident before the race, and we got a good break from the stalls. However, for the first three strides there was no pace, it was a nightmare. I was next to John Egan (on top-weight Lochbuie) and we both reacted quickly, we reined our horses back, and then everyone else took off and we ended up right at the back of the field.

"I went round with John and we were talking about how it had gone wrong. Because I was at the back of a 20-runner field I found trouble all the way round. It was only because of Cecil's quality and getting the luck of a run up the rail that he won the race. I was way too far back and shouldn't have been there."

Cooper couldn't see Munro's best-laid plans disintegrating because he couldn't

see very much at all. Reluctant to climb up into the stands because of the time it would take him to get down again after the race, he watched the action from the lawn near the rail, but there were so many people with the same idea his vision was all but obstructed. Millman, glued to his television at home, was wincing in sympathy at Munro's plight. "He pulled hard and was clipping heels everywhere he went," he says. "Alan had to pull him around a bit to keep him off the heels of the horses in front, and his head was going from side to side, everything went wrong. I knew then that whatever he did, whether he won or finished down the field, there was improvement to come because of what he had to go through. Alan gave him a great ride."

Cooper caught a glimpse of his vivid silks at the end of the back straight. "He was last. I saw him again a few seconds later and he was moving forward, but I didn't see any more until he'd gone past the post - there was a gap in the crowd and my colours flashed past. It looked like Cecil was in front but the angle didn't make it very easy to tell. I told myself not to jump up and down, not to make a fool of myself before I heard the result."

He must have been one of the few still to realise that Sergeant Cecil had done it. Notwithstanding his nightmare trip in the early stages, Munro had been able to get a good pitch on the rail and stuck to it like glue as Tungsten Strike towed the field along. From the three-furlong marker Munro prodded him closer, and then gaps began to appear as tired horses faded approaching the final furlong. In and out went the game

chestnut, flickering between his rivals like a tailor's needle until he hit the front in the last 100 yards and drew away from the toiling Tungsten Strike to win by a length and a half. The race was his well before Cooper saw him. Cooper didn't have to wait long for confirmation that he had at last won a big one. The result came booming out of the loudspeaker: "First, number 18, Sergeant Cecil . . ." It was Davey's first win with

Sergeant Cecil, and the pair went out on to the track to greet their conquering hero. "I went out on the track with Sue, and she took one side of him and I took the other," says Cooper. "I hate to see owners snatch a horse away from the groom and lead him in themselves, it's such bad manners - the grooms have done all the hard work and they want the horse to win just as much as the owner does, so they deserve a little moment in the limelight.

"My eyes welled up when we came into the winner's enclosure as the course announcer called out his name - Alan was over the moon and it was a shame Rod wasn't there, although he phoned up right after the race. I even coped okay when Derek Thompson interviewed me!

"While Cecil was being walked around, the chap I gave my spare badges to called out to me and I went over and shook his hand - he couldn't have been a nicer lad, and he wrote Sue and I a lovely letter a few days later thanking us."

It was Munro's biggest win since his return to Britain, and he said afterwards: "I'm delighted with the way things have turned out and I've loved every minute of it since I came back. Rod is not only a very good trainer, he's also a very good planner. Things didn't go too well for me early in the race, as I wanted to race in midfield from my draw but I kept getting knocked back - but I had all the luck going in the straight." The *Racing Post*'s Tom O'Ryan nominated Munro's performance as 'Ride of the Week'.

The very good trainer and very good planner, for whom the win was the most valuable of his career, the £104,000 first prize more than doubling all Cecil's previous earnings, laughs off the praise. "You might well ask what the hell was I doing before Newcastle," he says. "But it was a hell of a race to win, and I think the most important Cecil ever won as far as I was concerned, because it was the first big one and it took an awful lot of pressure off. I don't know about planning - with Cecil there weren't that many races he could go for anyway."

Sergeant Cecil and Alan Munro master Tungsten Strike and stride on to win the Northumberland Plate at Newcastle

Cooper's journey home was infinitely more serene, but he probably wouldn't have noticed had it been snowing frogs. "The drive home was wonderful, one of the best ever," he says. "I was on cloud nine - the day itself seemed to go so quickly and what was happening didn't really sink in at the time, so it just sank in gradually all the way home. When I got back Sue and my daughter Sam were there, so we opened a bottle of champagne and watched the replay, Sue and Sam telling me how they'd been jumping up and down screaming as Sergeant Cecil came through to win.

"Even now it was one of the best wins. It was a dream come true. We'd done it, and now everything was a bonus."

Cecil

# CHAPTER SIX

# THE OLD BUGGER'S ONLY GONE AND DONE IT AGAIN

In racing, there's generally no rest for the fast-improving, but Sergeant Cecil was allowed to bask in the luxury of an extra week with his feet up before returning to the fray. Millman had the Ebor firmly in his sights, but with the date of that race falling seven weeks after Newcastle, he wanted to give the gelding a run beforehand. The favoured path is generally the familiar one, and Sergeant Cecil went back to Goodwood for the valuable handicap in which he'd been runner-up to Mephisto 12 months earlier, although for some reason the race's value had been halved.

The Northumberland Plate had proved beyond doubt that Sergeant Cecil stayed two miles and could summon up a finishing kick at the end of it, but he dropped back two furlongs at Goodwood. Balkan Knight and Swift Sailor were in opposition again and the handicapper had raised Sergeant Cecil 4lb to a mark of 96, the highest of his career. As previously mentioned, luck plays an important part in races at Goodwood because a clear run through the field can never be relied upon, and hard-luck stories litter the course afterwards like so many torn-up betting slips.

Munro sought to counteract the inevitable bumping and barging by bringing Sergeant Cecil down the outside, as he had done at Epsom when third behind Crow Wood, but as in that race the horse flattened out through the final furlong as a result of being out in the open for too long. He finished third, a length and a half behind Golden Quest. Millman says: "Cecil wasn't the same as at Newcastle, he didn't quicken, he idled. But the main thing was that the race set the horse up nicely for York, and to be honest we weren't all that bothered about not picking up a penalty. We went there only because it suited our schedule."

Three weeks later, all roads led north to York for the Totesport-sponsored Ebor Handicap. Run over just a few yards shy of a mile and three-quarters, the Ebor is one of the most important handicaps in Britain and gives its name to the glittering three-day August meeting on the Knavesmire, so called because it was common ground and the site of the city's gallows until the start of the 19th century, with highwayman Dick Turpin the most celebrated victim of the hangman's craft. Run since 1843, the Ebor is the most valuable handicap in Europe and altogether a more prestigious contest than the Northumberland Plate.

There was another maximum field of 20, with the round-up of usual suspects bringing in the likes of Balkan Knight, Sendintank, Crow Wood, High Action, Defining and Swift Sailor, this time ignored by the betting public in favour of the David Elsworth-trained Balkan Knight. Elsworth must have looked at Sergeant Cecil in the parade ring and mused on what might have been, had he but followed up a certain phone call from a certain owner about a certain horse three years earlier. Newspaper tipsters looked elsewhere for their inspiration, although Sergeant Cecil, fifth choice in the betting market at 11-1, lacked no public support.

Millman had joined Cooper at the track, and as he watched Sergeant Cecil circle the parade ring on the arm of Sue Davey, he hedged his expectations. "The horse looked great in the sunshine, but I was watching him in the paddock and I just thought he'd lost a bit of his top line, a bit of his edge," he says.

"I gave Alan a leg-up and consoled myself by thinking 'ah well, at least we've already won a big one - the Plate's in the bag and everything else is a bonus.'"

Cooper, who had enjoyed a much more straightforward journey to the track than he had at Newcastle, was again without Sue, who was in hospital that day having another session of chemotherapy. That meant that he had badges going begging again and, as at Newcastle, he spread the Sergeant Cecil gospel with a gift to a stranger. He had a little local difficulty in finding a bed for the night, but eventually found a pub with rooms. "I had dinner in the pub and got chatting to a chap with a *Racing Post*, and of course he knew all about Cecil," he says. "He and his friend were going into Tattersalls, but I said that I'd leave a couple of badges at the owners' and trainers' gate so they could pick them up. The following morning I saw them at breakfast, when they just wanted to check that I hadn't had a few too many the previous night, and that I was who I said I was. They picked up their badges and had a lovely day, and a few days later they phoned to thank me for my generosity and sent Sue a big bunch of flowers as well.

"I spoke to Sue in hospital shortly after that, and she said that Cecil had been the Radio 4 tip of the day, just as he had been before the Plate. Their confidence was encouraging, but I told Sue that I really didn't think we'd be lucky enough to win both races."

Back at The Paddocks, Sharon Steel had remembered her long-range Ebor forecast of two years earlier, and was working herself up into a right state as the race drew nearer. Like trainer Henrietta Knight, who famously refused to watch any of Best Mate's three Cheltenham Gold Cup wins, Steel didn't intend to see a minute of the race and was relying on howls of joy or disappointment to bring her the result.

At York, the little knot of connections in the parade ring didn't have a great deal to say to each other. Munro knew what to expect from the horse, there were no worries about the ground or trip and there were no concerns about Sergeant

Cecil being up to the task after he had proved his mettle in the Plate. This time, there were no fuck-ups.

"Prior to this race, I had been on a journey of discovery with Cecil, and it was all a bit of a mess, but this was the one day when everything went to plan," says Munro. "He jumped out of the stalls and it was a much quicker race right from the start, so I was able to take him back and settle him into a nice position near the rear.

"I'd thought about the race beforehand and I had no anxiety about getting a run, because at that meeting they were tending to come up the middle of the track and I knew there would be plenty of gaps. It all worked perfectly. As we turned into the straight they all fanned out as I expected, so I just chose a path and deliberately, consciously took Cecil between horses rather than worrying about getting to the outside. There was a lot of room and we had a perfect run through."

Millman hadn't shared Munro's optimism in the early stages, but was warming to the gelding's progress as he scythed through the field. "It didn't go to plan completely, because I could see him wasting energy on the outside for the first furlong and a half, flinging his head around and being too keen. If he'd been beaten, that would have been the reason, but Alan eventually got him settled.

"Ideally, I'd have liked him to be more relaxed, and to have been able to sit closer. But it was a great run, obviously, and I was really chuffed to bits to win with Cecil after old Zibeline had finished fifth for me - the £130,000 prize-money was fantastic too."

Cooper had found himself a good spot to watch from, down by the rail, and followed the race on the big screen. "He looked good on the overhead shot, which made you realise how much ground he was making up. Then it got to the stage where you could see he was going to get there. Alan rode a brilliant race, faultless."

Jagger and Odiham had taken the field along at a strong pace, and as the 20 runners turned into the long straight Sergeant Cecil had only two or three behind him. Then the gaps started opening up before them, as did the Red Sea for Moses, and Munro fired him through. They came up the middle of the track, on the inside of the main group, but as they passed horses Munro always had cover ahead of him. Each rival passed gave Sergeant Cecil the impetus to roll on and catch the next, and as they reached the furlong pole the leaders were spread halfway across the track, the perfect scenario. Munro just had to make up his mind which route to take, and he angled through between Grampian and Zeitgeist. The little chestnut wriggled through the gap and buckled down under Munro's right-hand drive to take command in the last 100 yards, and although he may have idled in the final strides it mattered little, as he still had a length to spare over the staying-on Carte Diamond at the line.

Cooper, an inveterate screamer and shouter, let himself go in the last quarter-mile, and if anyone stared at him in bemusement he couldn't have cared less. "When he went past the post, I just couldn't believe it. I was back on cloud nine," he says. Similar screaming and shouting 230 miles away alerted Steel to the fact that she would be riding work on an Ebor winner in the next few days.

Millman and Munro dealt with the press enquiries - "This is probably our best win - the Ebor is a very famous race and I feel very proud. We'll probably go for Listed races now, or maybe the Doncaster Cup" and "It's beyond dreams

to pick up a horse like that in my first year back. It just keeps getting better this year" - leaving Cooper wandering happily befuddled around the winner's enclosure. He says: "I phoned Sue, who hadn't been able to watch the race in hospital, and my exact words to her were 'you're never going to guess, but the old bugger's only gone and done it again'. She'd been feeling sick all day with a drip in her arm, and she burst into tears. Cecil's a great one for cheering you up."

Davey was in the dope-test box, waiting for Sergeant Cecil to produce a sample. She knew she was in for a long wait. "He takes ages to have a pee in the dope box, and the vet generally has to take blood to do the test," she says. "Like everything, he's got a little routine. I plait his mane before the race, and he has a pee. I leave him, come back in an hour and a half, and he goes again. No wonder there's nothing left for the vet."

Every year a horse wins the Northumberland Plate, every year another horse wins the Ebor. There is nothing wonderfully remarkable, in the great scheme of racing, about winning either race, but what Sergeant Cecil did at York lifted him above the ordinary in everyone's eyes, not just those of his nearest and dearest. No horse had won both Plate and Ebor since Pillo did the double in 1911, and only two others - Victor Emmanuel (1882) and Underhand (1859) - had done it at all. It's possible that few had tried, but it is testament to the outright near-impossibility of such a feat that only four had achieved it in more than 160 years. His double strike had assured him both public and media interest - wherever he went next, journalists and racegoers would follow in his wake.

The Ebor win marked a shift in the perception of Sergeant Cecil. From this point on his popularity soared, and he edged ever further into the public domain. He wasn't in Arkle, Desert Orchid and Red Rum territory - he had barely made the back page, let alone the front page, and no-one was singing songs about him - but he was a firm favourite with armchair racing fans and was building a following in the internet

Cecil and Munro have too much in the tank for Carte Diamond and Grampian (pink silks)

chatrooms. Few Flat horses inspire such affection; jumpers are generally the ones to exert an emotional pull. He was becoming a phenomenon - he even had his own website: www.sergeant-cecil.com.

Cooper drove home in a state of bliss, his wheels barely touching the tarmac. Sue was at home to greet him, and Don Hazzard - on a high with another £3,000 breeder's prize in the bag - joined them for a drop of midnight champagne. Celebrations lose their edge when postponed by sleep, so Cooper makes a point, whatever the hour, of raising a glass or three to Sergeant Cecil after every success. "The previous year we thought we had a little star," he says. "Now he's a superstar. It's simply out of this world."

## Up for the Cup

It didn't take the racing press long to wax lyrical about their new darling. The *Racing Post*'s Mark Blackman awarded the accolade of 'Training performance of the Week' to Millman, writing: ". . . goes to Rod Millman for the success of Sergeant Cecil in the staying handicap that gives the York fixture its name.

"It takes a good piece of training to win one major handicap in a season, let alone two, so for the Devon handler to bring the Northumberland Plate hero all the way back up to plunder another huge northern prize rates a serious exhibition of talent, as it takes a fine bit of long-term training to bring even a slow-maturing horse to a new peak at that age.

"Understandably, much of the attention after the Ebor centred on Alan Munro, whose return to the fray this year has brought a fascinating narrative to the campaign. At the start of the season, Munro suggested he'd need 100 rides to reach his peak - and there's no question his riding in a finish is right back to its best now."

In the same paper, Alastair Down nailed his colours to the mast in his column, ending on a note that was beginning to ring true for many followers of the sport. He wrote: "But for me, the star of day two was Sergeant Cecil. We are used to the occasional bang-in-form sprinter notching a Wokingham-Stewards' Cup double or, having taken the Goodwood event, adding the Ayr Gold Cup for good measure. But Sergeant Cecil plies his trade in altogether stormier waters. The Ebor winner is just about the definition of the Flat horse I'd most like to own."

While Sergeant Cecil recovered from his Ebor exertions - Davey says: "When he comes back after a race, he's a nightmare. He takes two weeks to settle back into his routine. After that I find him very good." - Millman took stock of the possibilities open to him. The handicapper's opinion of Sergeant Cecil's progress was a rise in the ratings of 8lb to a mark of 104, which to all intents and purposes excluded him from all handicaps except the two he had just won and the Cesarewitch. The only viable option was to introduce him into the Pattern system, in which he would be taking on the best stayers in Britain and Europe. Was he good enough to bridge the gap between handicap company and Group races? Many before had looked good enough, only to be found wanting when harsh reality took over from optimistic theory.

Millman thumbed through the programme book, a pastime that often occupied Cooper for an idle hour as he formulated possibilities for forthcoming destinations. There were fewer options now for Sergeant Cecil - the better a horse gets, the more clearly defined its career path becomes - but one race leapt out of the pages immediately. Three weeks after York comes Doncaster, and the Group 2 Doncaster Cup over two and a quarter miles, mentioned by Millman in the heat of the moment after the Ebor victory, now looked the right option.

It meant Sergeant Cecil would have to stretch his stamina to an extra two furlongs, but set against that was the likelihood of a small field and a steady pace. In his earlier incarnation that might have spelled disaster, but now he had evolved as a racehorse, gaining racecraft and confidence and a jockey whose tactical awareness was perfectly suited to gleaning the utmost from his complicated partner. As to the gulf in quality between handicappers and Group horses, Millman had the answer. "Group horses tend to try harder than handicappers," he says. "That's what separates them, not natural ability or the trainer's ability. They are willing to push back the pain barrier, if you like, and dig deeper into their resources than horses who can't make that leap out of handicaps." There was little doubt that Sergeant Cecil was of that calibre - but one thing connections couldn't control was the weather.

It rained all over Town Moor in the hours leading up to the Cup, saturating the ground and ensuring a slog for the seven runners. The official going description of 'good' was some way removed from the actual conditions - "A joke, it had to be nearer heavy," says Munro - and Sergeant Cecil was guaranteed not to be impressed. "The ground was horrible, sloppy and sticky," says Millman. "But we knew we would be able to hold him up, and with just a handful of runners he'd be close to the pace rather than miles off it. The tactical question was whether we followed Millenary. If we followed him and he was on a non-going day it would put us in trouble, so I left it to Alan to see how things went."

In a neat inversion of the norm, Cooper admits he was thrilled to bits even before the race, delighted that he had a horse with the talent to have a distinct chance in a Group 2. Sergeant Cecil was third-favourite behind Distinction and 2000 St Leger winner Millenary, on whose enthusiasm the race hinged.

Sergeant Cecil settled at the rear of the field, a place ahead of Millenary, on whom Richard Quinn was utilising the most patient of waiting tactics. Munro takes up the story. "Millenary was following me, and for the whole way round we were racing with hardly any cover but he switched right off, he knew how to run a race. He had developed over the last few races an understanding of a race pattern, and it made such a big difference.

"Coming round the last turn I started to wake him up and he was responsive. He was brilliant - he responded, but in a measured way, a half-hearted way. He knew that it wasn't time to give everything yet, he was getting to know that we weren't at the crucial stage of a race, he was beginning almost to time things for me. A few runs earlier he would have flattened out, but not this new Cecil.

"We went to win the race and I was thinking we had it, but Millenary came incredibly late and beat us. Even though we were beaten, I was really pleased with the way he ran because he defied two things that we thought were beyond him - the soft ground and his former habit of flattening out, as this time he produced a finish even though he'd been in the firing line a long time."

It was no disgrace to be beaten by Millenary, and by only three-quarters of a length at that, as it was the evergreen horse's eleventh Group-race success and his second Doncaster Cup. Sergeant Cecil clearly had the class for Group races, and if the weather had been on his side he might well have won one at the first time of asking. Millman says: "It would have been closer on fast ground but it was a great run, although he had a hard

Millenary (blinkers) comes through to collar
Sergeant Cecil in the dying strides at Doncaster

race, slogging through the mud." It was a great run, the best of the horse's career despite defeat. It was also a great ride from Quinn on the winner.

## Three is the magic number

There was one more race in Sergeant Cecil that autumn, and it would be at Newmarket on Champions Day - but Millman had a choice to make. Most observers would consider his dilemma no choice at all - where would the merit lie in contesting the Group 2 Jockey Club Cup instead of attempting to reconfigure the history books in the Cesarewitch? - but Millman's remit was to give Sergeant Cecil the best possible chance to win a race, and if he thought the Cup was the best spot then he would have been doing the right thing by running him in it.

"There were two races," he says. "In the Jockey Club Cup, you would have to ask yourself whether he could beat Millenary, and he would have a hard race even if he could. In the Cesarewitch, he was obviously ahead of his handicap mark because he'd just finished second in a Group race, and we knew he'd stay the trip whereas three-quarters of the field wouldn't. However, they'd get in his way, he'd have to fight his way through them, and it wouldn't be easy. But he was a good thing for the Cesarewitch if he didn't get boxed in, and when I discovered that no horse had ever won all three it helped to make my mind up.

"There was no pressure on us, because we'd already won two huge races - I never dreamed we'd win them - and it was more of a carnival atmosphere at Newmarket. We went there to enjoy the race."

There was a fever of anticipation hanging over the Totesport-sponsored race, ostensibly one of the lesser races on a glittering card that featured two Group 1s but because of circumstance the most eagerly awaited. The Cesarewitch had first been run in 1839 and required horses to start in one county (Cambridgeshire) and finish in another (Suffolk), in between running for two and a quarter miles across the soul-destroying expanse of Newmarket heath. It was a pitiless race.

No horse had won the Northumberland Plate, Ebor and Cesarewitch before - the three to attempt the treble had all been beaten at Newmarket. It was the kind of feat that was barely discussed because of its impossibility. Here were three of the toughest races in the calendar, run at a variety of trips over a four-month period, with the handicapper allowed to have his say between each race and a huge number of rivals invariably in opposition. Horses just didn't do the treble; pigs didn't fly.

Sergeant Cecil had 9st 8lb to carry, top weight when Adam Kirby's 5lb claim was subtracted from True Lover's 9st 10lb, which was a far cry from his Plate success when he squeezed in at the bottom of the weights. Unusually for such a brutally competitive contest, the favourite, the Nicky Henderson-trained Afrad, was as short as 3-1. Sergeant Cecil was third choice at 10-1 to beat 33 rivals and make history; there can't have been a soul at Newmarket that day, not immediately connected with one of the other runners, who didn't want the old chestnut to win.

Cooper was there, Sue had finished her chemotherapy and was there, as was Ian, Cooper's eldest son from his first marriage. Neville Poole had come up with them. Cooper's brother-in-law and his son were there - no need for Cooper to donate his owner's badges to a good cause this time. Millman was there, chirpy as ever and fending off the myriad media interviews. Jack Micklem was there, keeping a close eye on proceedings, Davey was there, keeping a close eye on Sergeant Cecil. Munro was there, cool as a cucumber, mentally running through potential mid-race scenarios and preparing himself for every eventuality. They made a hopeful little band in the parade ring, Cooper feeling the pressure, Millman and Munro more collected, calm in the face of the task awaiting them.

Munro laughs: "How could we ever think he was going to win the Cesarewitch? I wasn't feeling any pressure. Terry came up to me in the paddock, put his hand on my shoulder and said 'look, my boy' - he always calls me 'boy' - 'whatever happens, just enjoy it, and bring him back in one piece'. He's a great owner to ride for.

"We all knew the horse's requirements by now, but the thing to think about this time was whether I took him to the back or kept him closer to the pace, because there were so many runners. We were drawn high (28, on the far rail) so I made up my mind to put him somewhere in the middle of the field."

Cooper had already been shanghaied by Nick Luck to do an interview for Racing UK, and now he found Derek Thompson confronting him with a microphone for the Channel 4 viewers. Already a bag of nerves, all Cooper wanted to do was watch his horse canter to post, and consequently gave what he confesses was "the worst interview ever". Back in Kentisbeare, Sharon Steel didn't see Sergeant Cecil go down either, although that was through choice. "He'd been well up for it before the race," she says. "The day before a race he does one steady work, not two, and I usually have to take him in the yard because he wants to be on the gallop while the others go up again, and he really lets you know. The day before the Cesarewitch he was such a handful I had to put him back in his box."

The 34 runners left the stalls in a multicoloured wave. Munro was immediately gratified to find that there was plenty of pace, and he tucked Sergeant Cecil in towards the rail about two-thirds of the way back. He says: "I decided to follow Kieren Fallon (on Afrad) and Seb Sanders (Elusive Dream), because I knew those two horses would keep going and those boys are good riders to follow anyway." From the packed stands, about two miles distant, his manoeuvring was practically invisible. Watching racing at Newmarket is unsatisfactory at the best of times, with horses running straight towards the stands through the final mile and a quarter. Those without binoculars gaze at the big screen, and with 34 slightly blurry brownish horses involved, identification is not easy. Cooper was not finding it easy despite his easy-to-spot spotted silks.

"I lost track of him in the race," he says. "When the field turned for home there were a couple tailed off, and one looked a bit like my colours. I thought 'uh oh, he's had a long season, something's gone wrong' and asked Neville if he could see him, and then half a minute or so later he appeared through a gap."

It was a rough race. There was a right old cavalry charge coming down the Rowley Mile like a swarm of bees, jockeys jostling for position and horses running into pockets, clipping heels and abruptly changing course. Munro was still over towards the far rail, around ten or fifteen horses back, and the shape of the race was changing. With half a mile to run the non-stayers began to cry enough, dropping back through the field as those with plenty left to give began to come through. It was what Millman had been worried about,

but approaching the quarter-mile marker, Munro saw his chance.

"Luckily, at the two-furlong pole a gap opened up on the left and he was able to get out and show his brilliant turn of foot," he says. "When he picked up, I knew he would get there. I watched the replay and it was amazing, it looked like he wasn't under any pressure. The Ebor and Cesarewitch went perfectly right. He was the most professional he'd ever been at Newmarket - the long canter to post, all the traffic, always on the heels of the horses in front - he was great, he handled it brilliantly."

In the stands, Cooper wasn't so confident, but unlike Munro he couldn't feel the mighty warrior flexing his muscles and easing through the gears. "He pulled out to challenge and he was about fourth, and I didn't think we were going to win," says Cooper. "Then, as he moved forward, I thought he is going to win, he moved into second and looked really strong. He really stretched and put everything into it."

Sergeant Cecil emerged from the scrum of horses and Munro drove him down into the Dip. He passed two horses on the way and had only King Revo ahead of him, but the leader had the rail to help him and was running on strongly. But Munro knew he would get there, because he knew Sergeant Cecil. The horse had come a long way to get where he was at that precise moment, and had touched the lives of many people on the journey.

Don Hazzard, sitting in front of his television with a glass of brandy at home in the village of Mere, thought of the day he bought the mare Jadidh at the sale-ring no more than a mile or two down the road from Newmarket racecourse, and the day Arthur Barrow phoned up and told him he had a fine chestnut colt foal. Seamus Mullins, Lou Griffin and Alison Dunford thought back to the day Sergeant Cecil arrived at the yard, tottering down from the horsebox on his yearling legs, and the day he wore the stalls-handlers out with his effortless obstinacy. Sharon Steel, nowhere near a television and waiting impatiently for someone to tell her the result, remembered the

No.3 in the bag - Cecil
conquers King Revo

day Sergeant Cecil arrived at The Paddocks, and the wild mornings that followed as she fought to smooth away his rough-edged exuberance and instil him with patience and practicality. Sue Davey thought of the endless hours of feeding, grooming, cleaning, brushing and washing, talking to her boy in a soft murmur as she shone his coat to a mirror sheen. Rod Millman remembered the first time he'd seen the gelding, reckoning that he could win a race or two with him; Neville Poole thought of the short winter afternoons watching Sergeant Cecil at leisure, growing strong bone and clean limbs on the Paradise Farm chalkland; Terry and Sue Cooper thought of the disappointing early days of ownership, and the gradual dawning down the years that by some stroke of magic they had a horse in a million, in ten million.

Alan Munro might have thought of the years away from racing and how this horse had helped him to return home like a prodigal son, if he hadn't been more occupied by three lengths to make up and a furlong in which to do so. He asked his horse for what he knew he had in him, and they came up the hill into history. Sergeant Cecil flattened out like a greyhound and Munro mirrored him, crouching low in the style he learned and made his own half a lifetime earlier. As encouragement came crashing down from the stands in a great wash of joyful noise, Sergeant Cecil caught King Revo, passed him and strode away on his own. There was no stopping him now. He crossed the line three-quarters of a length clear, the horse who made the impossible treble possible.

"The applause from the stands was incredible," says Cooper. "Everyone was jumping up and down, shouting and screaming - I was shouting and screaming all right. Neville was two or three steps below me, and when Cecil went over the line we jumped into each other's arms and everyone looked at us - we're not gays or anything, you know, we're both married! I can't describe the thrill of that little horse winning that race.

"Somehow I got down from the stands and ran up the course to congratulate Alan. I grabbed his hand and shook it, and he kept saying 'we've made history, you know, we've made history'. He must have said it three or four times, he was caught up in it as much as I was."

The crowd moved as one towards the winner's enclosure, swarming through the concourse to get there as quickly as possible so as to greet the history-makers as they returned to unsaddle. In a contest to find the happiest man on the racecourse, Millman was in a multiple dead-heat. "The reception when he came in was amazing," he says. "Cecil had the biggest cheer of all, more than the Champion Stakes winner half an hour before. It was a fantastic feeling, it made me so proud, and it was wonderful for Alan in his first season back - he really took the horse up to another level."

In the maelstrom of the winner's enclosure, he told the assembled press pack: "We were thinking about the Jockey Club Cup, but when I was told that no-one has ever done the treble, I thought let's try it. It was wonderful just to have been able to have a crack and unbelievable to have actually achieved it.

"The credit has to go to a good horse, good staff and a good jockey. I've been at the sales all week but the horse has been in safe hands at home under my head groom Jim Davies, and Alan has been amazing and rides this horse so well. He needs a confident jockey on him and someone who isn't going to panic if he gets boxed in. The Doncaster Cup was really a bit of an afterthought, but now we shall have to start thinking about the Cup races for him next season."

The next race was due off, and it was time for the Sergeant Cecil team to box him up and go home. Munro had no time to celebrate his win as he had packing to do and the decorators coming on the Monday, so he had plenty to sort out at home, but Millman and Cooper and their friends and family headed west as the events of an unparalleled day began to sink slowly in. Millman flicked on the radio as he drove home, tuning in to Radio 5. "Cecil was all over the radio," he said. "They were talking about him and saying what a wonderful feat it was, and it really made me feel proud of what we'd achieved. Then I turned my phone back on and texts came flooding through, full of congratulations for me and the staff. It was a wonderful drive home."

Cooper took the same route, delighted with the day and even more so because Sue had been there to experience it with him. "It was absolutely fantastic, another dream day. On the way home, it really began to sink in that he had made history, so when we got back we phoned Don - he'd won another big breeder's prize, of course - and he came over and we opened a bottle or two. The Ebor had been the aim, the Plate was totally unexpected, and no-one could have imagined we'd win the Cesarewitch too. I wanted to win a big one, but instead I won three . . ." his voice tails away in happy incredulity.

If this story had been made up, you wouldn't have believed it.

# CHAPTER SEVEN

# IT WASN'T GOING TO BE EASY

Sergeant Cecil had done enough for the season - for any season - and the papers were full of his glorious achievement. Scrapbook compilers sent out for more midnight oil and put in the overtime, as words of praise, admiration and delight came tumbling out of the presses.

In the *Independent on Sunday*, Sue Montgomery wrote: "Sergeant Cecil, the horse named as a monument to a soldier, proved himself a valiant warrior without peer here yesterday. By adding victory in the Cesarewitch to triumphs in the Northumberland Plate and Ebor, the six-year-old became the first horse in history to win the calendar's three top staying handicaps in the same season. The story of the gallant chestnut gelding has been a grass-roots Turf inspiration."

The *Racing Post* again awarded 'Training performance of the Week' to Millman with the words: ". . . Sergeant Cecil is this remarkable animal, winner of the Northumberland Plate, Ebor and, last Saturday, the Cesarewitch, becoming the first horse in the long histories of the three races to bring off the hat-trick. The six-year-old gelding has been prepared to perfection by former journeyman jump jockey Rod Millman, who has nursed his charge up through the handicap from a rating of 92 at Newcastle in June to success off 104 at Newmarket at the weekend.

"On Saturday, Millman said: "The credit has to go to a good horse, good staff and a good jockey." Some of the credit, anyway. But most of it has to go to Millman, who has gleaned every grain of ability from his big-hearted stable star."

The following year, in the latest of the *Racing Post*'s '100 Greatest' series, readers of the paper were to vote Millman's feat in harvesting the three big handicaps with the same horse to be the 37th greatest training performance of all time.

Other writers went further. Alastair Down, the *Post*'s pre-eminent colour writer, sewed his heart to his sleeve and waved it around for all to see in his report from

Champions Day. The headline read 'Get here nine o'clock sharp Monday morning, I need a shrine to Sergeant Cecil in the corner of the sitting room. I'll buy the candles' and the copy encompassed what the horse had done for racing and what it could now do for him, the fag-end of the year being the time for cigars and champagne and awards dinners. Down wrote: "Ask racegoers leaving Newmarket late Saturday afternoon which of the 108 runners they would most like to take home with them, and those with half a brain, or even a smattering of red corpuscles in their veins, would chorus one name and one only - Sergeant Cecil.

"We race horses to test many aspects of the thoroughbred, and among them have to be durability, willingness, courage and plain old ability. In Sergeant Cecil we have a one-off. He is that utter rarity, the stayer with a telling turn of foot or a gear change at the very stage, around two miles, that every other horse is red-lining it and finding nothing. I'll concede to the purists that he is not pure class, but he is a pure class act. Nothing fazes him and he loves the hurly-burly and traffic that sours so many.

Sergeant Cecil would never get stuck on the M25 in the rush hour, he'd always find a way through and get there on time.

"The forthcoming Cartier Awards don't cater for the likes of Sergeant Cecil, but readers of this paper do have a say in who wins the *Racing Post*/Racehorse Owners' Horse of the Year Award in December, and if this entirely admirable, covetable and loveable beau ideal of a stayer doesn't win it, then we are indeed losing touch with what a true star is. And what racing should be about."

There are several awards ceremonies at the end of each year. Some own considerably more prestige than others, but the *Racing Post*/Racehorse Owners' Association Awards are up there with the best of them and, given that the destination of the award for Horse of the Year is jointly decided by readers of the *Racing Post* and members of the ROA, that award proves a good litmus test of public opinion.

There were six contenders for the Horse of the Year award - Derby winner Motivator, Cheltenham Gold Cup winner Kicking King, Prix de l'Arc de Triomphe winner Hurricane Run, World Hurdle winner Inglis Drever, Champion Chase hero Moscow Flyer and Sergeant Cecil. *Racing Post* writers made a case for each of the six, and the votes rolled in.

It was a landslide. Sergeant Cecil polled almost twice as many votes as the runner-up, and Cooper received the award on what is customarily described as 'a glittering evening' at the Park Lane Hilton in London. It was a very proud moment for Cooper and his family and friends, and something of an eye-opener for Millman, for whom the approval of his peers was thoroughly unexpected and much appreciated. He says: "It was a hell of a night, they're our Oscars, of course. But so many trainers came up to me to offer their congratulations - trainers can be a bit lofty

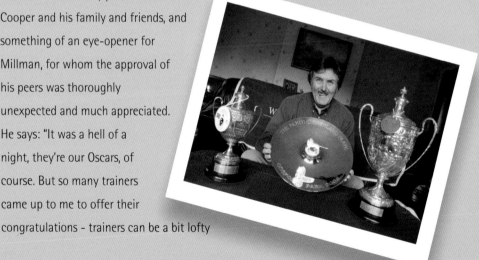

sometimes, we're all in our own little world and don't really take that much notice of other people's horses - and I had trainers I didn't even know coming up to shake my hand.

"I didn't realise just how other people felt about the horse. He doesn't get any special treatment here, we try just as hard to win a race with the most moderate of our horses as we do with him, but it was lovely to see so many others pleased for us and pleased for him. It meant a hell of a lot and made me think about the impact he had on other people, whether in racing or not. Even our local racetrack Exeter - and Flat racing is usually a dirty word at Haldon - named a race after Cecil: the Sergeant Cecil Triple Victory Novices' Handicap Chase."

Chris Deuters, president of the Racehorse Owners' Association, said: "I was pleased that Sergeant Cecil won as it was a unique achievement to win the three races he did, and no disrespect to the equine bluebloods, but on this occasion the ROA members seemed to have voted with their hearts. I was delighted for Rod Millman. He's a softly-spoken, modest man and it couldn't have happened to a nicer person."

Sergeant Cecil also earned his place in *Flat Horses of 2005*, published by the *Racing Post*, which had previously concerned itself only with the cream of world thoroughbreds. A Group 1 win was the only way in which to gain admittance, but for such an achievement as Sergeant Cecil's the book's editorial 'bouncers' turned a blind eye and threw the door wide open for racing's newest hero, writing: "'What's he doing in here? This book is for Group 1 winners - Classic heroes, sprint kings, magical milers. Look, old chap, it's just not done to let the rank and file in. Dam was a hurdler, I hear. Not our type at all. Handicapper, you know'.

"He may be a little too blue-collar for the bluebloods, but Sergeant Cecil's exploits in 2005 entitled him to look anyone in the eye. No horse has ever done what Sergeant Cecil did: win the three great staying handicaps - Northumberland Plate, Ebor and

caption

Cesarewitch - in the same season. The ranks of staying handicappers are generally characterised by plenty of guts and precious little glory - rarely mentioned in dispatches and often dismissed as betting-shop cannon-fodder. That was Sergeant Cecil when the season started - by its end he was front-page news.

"Sergeant Cecil has rather run himself out of handicaps, so the Cup route may become a necessity next season. His detractors may have damned him hitherto with the badge of 'handicapper', but he wore that badge like a medal and won himself a lasting place in Turf history. The story may not be over; 2006 may bring him a Group 1 garnish and a place in these pages by right. Sergeant Cecil, we salute you."

But the simplest tribute came from Emma Lavelle, who as capricious coincidence would have it trains from the Andover yard where Seamus Mullins began his training career. When asked by the *Racing Post* to provide her highlight of 2005, she replied: "I think the highlight of 2005 was Sergeant Cecil and all that he achieved - it gave hope for us all that you can find a top horse."

## Realism, not romanticism

The new year dawned with three historic trophies on Cooper's mantelpiece and the future wide open. Those trophies weren't required to be returned for the next lucky owner to brandish in delight, so the satisfying sweep of silver and glass above the fireplace is a permanent reminder of an incredible season. They need regular dusting, but the extra housework is never seen as a problem.

Sergeant Cecil had spent the winter at Paradise Farm Stud, as was his custom, but this little holiday provided its own anxieties and underlined the fact that where racehorses were concerned, even the slightest nicks and bruises can provoke alarm bells given their fragility. Cooper also had a two-year-old with Millman, a Piccolo filly named Suesam after his wife and daughter, who had won a Newbury maiden in June and finished fifth to no less a future star than Sir Percy on her next outing. Suesam was also a boarder at Paradise, and the two travelled together on the short journey from Kentisbeare, a journey that gave the two time to bond.

Cooper says: "Both Rod and Neville warned me against it, but this winter, instead of turning him out on his own, we put them in neighbouring paddocks. That was all well and good, but the layout of the filly's paddock enabled her to go where Cecil couldn't see her, and he thought he'd been left on his own. That worried him and he couldn't rest, he was wearing himself out going around the field, so I gave in and put the filly in with him.

"That solved one problem but created another - although Cecil is a gelding he still has a colty nature, and he kept biting the mare on the backside. She wasn't particularly taken with the attention and lashed out a few times, catching him on the front legs and leaving a few marks. It was giving me nightmares - I never knew whether I'd come up to see him one day and find a big chunk out of his leg - so I was glad to send them back to Rod's, glad to see the back of him."

Back at The Paddocks, with his misplaced ardour cooling, work began in preparation for another busy season, and Millman appreciated that this would be a hard year for his stable star, whose exploits had now forced him into the high-octane cut and thrust of Group races from the word go. With his first run always no more than a pipe-opener, a five-finger exercise before reaching concert pitch, Millman decided to drop him back in distance to a mile and a half in the Group 3 John Porter Stakes at Newbury. "We'd got him pretty fit, although he was still a bit heavy," he says. "We knew he needed the race in any case."

Munro says: "We knew the race was too short, but we still wanted to keep him in his race pattern and therefore didn't want to push him along too early. We knew he'd be out the back, the idea was to get him to finish well. As things turned out he ran a blinder. I brought him down the outside from a long way back in a race run at no more than a reasonable gallop, he finished fourth behind some good horses, and I was delighted with that for a first run."

Cooper was "thrilled to bits (again!), he was going forward nicely at the finish", and although Sergeant Cecil could never land a blow at the winner, the well-loved veteran and Newbury specialist Mubtaker, Millman took as consolation the fact that he had proved he still retained his ability and had earned "a couple of grand for having a gallop round, which I thought wasn't bad".

For his next run Sergeant Cecil went back to York, scene of his Ebor triumph, for the Group 2 Yorkshire Cup over the same trip. Away from a mile and a half the fields tend to be smaller and the opposition not quite so blessed with strength in depth, and only seven eventually went to post after three late withdrawals because of the very soft ground. It was nearly four. "Terry and I drove up in the morning and we had a long chat about pulling him out," says Millman. "There had already been a couple taken out,

Percussionist (centre) sloshes through the mud to beat Sergeant Cecil and Alan Munro in the Yorkshire Cup

which left me leaning towards running Cecil because the race was cutting up - it looked easier without Collier Hill and Day Flight in opposition."

With Sergeant Cecil already at the track, the decision was made to run, especially as Munro was sure to look after him should the state of the ground prove insurmountable. The 'mire' part of the Knavesmire is not a misleading description - when the ground is very soft it resembles quicksand, sucking the strength out of a horse's legs and dragging under the best-laid plans of trainers and punters alike.

"The ground was similar to that at Doncaster for the Cup the previous year," says Munro. "It was very soft indeed, but I thought he'd overcome the bad going when coming to win his race a furlong or so out until Percussionist pulled out more in the closing stages - Cecil didn't stop but Percussionist loves that ground and was in his element. At that level, and on that ground, it was a brilliant effort by Cecil."

Millman agreed, although adding the caveat that realism rather than romanticism would underpin Sergeant Cecil's seven-year-old campaign following the heady days of the previous year. "Percussionist was a better horse on the day and in those conditions, but in coming second we won £30,000, which paid for the horse for the rest of the season.

"But the thing a lot of people had to remember was that Cecil was seven years old and was having to improve again to be competitive at this level, which is not something a lot of seven-year-olds are capable of. Physically, he still had plenty left, because he's only ever run when he's right and has never been abused, and when he hasn't won he hasn't had a hard race because his style of running lends itself to that - he's not a front-runner who puts his neck on the line in every race.

"But a lot of people thought he'd easily step up to the next level after the season he had in 2005, which is a romantic view of the situation. We took a more pragmatic view, the truth being that it would be hard to bridge the gap. We knew it wasn't going to be easy."

A look at Sergeant Cecil's rivals in the Yorkshire Cup bears that out. The three-length winner Percussionist had finished fourth in North Light's Derby (although he had already won over hurdles and would go on to do the same over fences), while fourth-placed Kastoria would later win the Irish St Leger, fifth home The Geezer had been runner-up in the St Leger the previous year, and Cherry Mix, who was sixth, had been runner-up in the 2004 Arc. These were not handicappers. There would be nowhere for Sergeant Cecil to hide should he be found wanting - and with an official rating of 112 there was no going back to handicaps. It was onwards and hopefully upwards - and the next test would be the toughest yet.

"The Gold Cup, top hat and tails time," smiles Cooper. "Disaster time!" Cooper is not a morning suit type, but then most sensible people aren't. "I enjoyed the Pitmen's Derby more, because it was more laid-back, more casual - I'm not one for strutting about in a top hat." He's not one for the attendant hype either, which goes double for Sharon Steel and Sue Davey, who say almost in unison: "The only downside to having Cecil is all the extra attention. Obviously it was always going to happen, as his profile got bigger, but all that extra fuss is no fun for us." Steel adds, wistfully: "I remember him when he came here. He was my little baby then, and I can't help but feel a bit jealous now that everyone wants to know all about him. Sometimes it feels like I've lost him to the rest of the world."

Cooper says: "The BBC cameras went to Rod's - Rishi Persad came down to interview us - but I just thought there was too much build-up and pressure put on the whole Cecil team for that particular race. A lot of people seemed to think he was going to win it, but we all felt that it was a big step up again - a Group 1 race, an extra two furlongs - and I just had a feeling that it was going to go pear-shaped. It generally does after too much hype. I always think you should do things first and jump up and down about it afterwards, get it done before you start talking about it.

"Before the race I told Rod that I didn't think the horse was fit. He'd put a bit of weight on, and it had been five weeks since his previous run, which I think was too long. He just had too much of a belly. And as for the new Ascot . . . don't get me started. All things considered, the day went exactly how I'd feared it would."

The Ascot Gold Cup is the holy grail for stayers. Its fortunes waned considerably in the late 1980s and early 1990s, prompting calls for the race to be reborn at a shorter trip in a bid to attract a different type of horse, but since then, and without any changes, the quality and quantity of runners has increased pleasingly, to the extent that it is now once again one of the highlights of the royal meeting. It was testament to Sergeant Cecil's progress that he was third favourite, a place ahead of the high-class mile-and-a-half horse Yeats, who had won the Coronation Cup the previous year but was making his seasonal reappearance over a trip three-quarters

Charlie, the Millmans' mascot

142

of a mile further than anything he had tried before. Also in the field were Melbourne Cup hero Media Puzzle and old rivals Tungsten Strike and High Action.

Unfortunately, Cooper's misgivings were justified. Sergeant Cecil was keen in the early stages behind a steady pace, and once Munro got him settled he decided to follow Frankie Dettori aboard Guadalajara. "I was behind Frankie on the rails, getting a good run round," says the jockey. "As we turned for home, Frankie's horse was bumped, and in turn he gave Cecil a bump and we lost momentum. All credit to Cecil, he reacted quickly, but by the time we picked ourselves up and got going again the race was basically over."

Yeats had skipped clear, and with his mile-and-a-half speed allied to evident staying power he turned the race into a one-horse parade, drawing away to beat Reefscape by four lengths. It was a mighty performance, one of the best seen in a Gold Cup for some years, and Sergeant Cecil was not disgraced in taking fifth place, especially as it was plain he was not at his best and had also endured a troubled passage. Millman says: "It was all a bit of an anti-climax, especially when you consider all the hype that had gone before. Cecil usually beats High Action but that one finished a place ahead of him - Yeats was unbeatable on the day but I think a peak-form Cecil would have finished second."

The day was ruined completely when the gallant Media Puzzle had to be put down after breaking down irreparably in the closing stages. For Cooper, it was all a bit too close to home. "We all know what can happen with racehorses, knowing how easy it is for things to go wrong, and I just felt so sorry for the poor horse and his connections - it was a 'there but for the grace of God' moment," he says. "It was a day best forgotten, I was glad to get out of the place."

With half the year gone, it was time for the calendar to tilt in Sergeant Cecil's favour. Millman knew the gelding came into his own in the second half of the year,

Land N'Stars gets back up on the line to beat Sergeant Cecil and Alan Munro at Sandown

and twice before he had won a race in the first ten days of July. Almost three weeks after the Gold Cup, Millman thought he had found the ideal race in which to get the horse back in the winning groove and act as a springboard to a lucrative autumn.

In the run-up to the race, a Listed contest over two miles at Sandown, Millman told the *Racing Post*: "On some of his form he ran about 4lb below his best at Ascot, and I think the last couple of furlongs just caught him out. He just came off the bridle a bit too soon. But if someone told me he was going to finish fifth in a Gold Cup 12 months ago, I would have said they were mad.

Land N'Stars, just too quick for Cecil today

"We thought we'd run him here because everything else we have planned for him will be at Group level, so this could be one for him to get his head in front."

It should have been, but what was that old line about best-laid plans? There were only five runners and Sergeant Cecil, for the first and only time in his career, was an odds-on favourite, but long-distance races with few runners can prove annoyingly tactical affairs, and there is much more scope for things to go wrong than might meet the eye. Munro, who recalls the day with particular clarity, provides a good description of the changing fortunes of the race. "We didn't go that quickly, it was a funny little race," he says. "Coming down the hill with just under a circuit to run, Ted Durcan (on Barolo) eased off the rail and left me a big gap, and with no cover Cecil then started to race a bit keenly.

"Turning for home there were three in front of me - John Egan (Winged D'Argent) who'd kicked and gone four lengths clear, Durcan under pressure on my left and Paul Doe (Land N'Stars) pushing the head off his on my right. So I'm thinking I've got two beaten and half a mile to make up four lengths on the one in front. I'm on a horse with a turn of foot, it's looking good.

"I'm doing it gradually, because I don't want to get there too soon and risk Cecil idling, I'm timing it to get to John inside the final furlong. However, between the two pole and the furlong marker Land N'Stars came back into it, and I wasn't keeping an eye on him. As I get to John, Paul gets a great run up the rail and does us both. I never actually got to the front. I should have won the race - it was a shame."

A neck was all there was in it, but the *Racing Post*'s race analyst noted: "Last year's horse of the year is certainly finding it hard, having had to step out of handicaps into Pattern races, and certainly has not been helped by some tactical races not playing to his strengths."

When would it all come together for Sergeant Cecil? Would it at all? Those dewy-eyed romantics who, at the start of the season, had been expecting the horse to continue to sweep all before him in a higher grade were now wondering whether they had seen the best of him. With his placed efforts in Group company he had exceeded his handicap form, but many had expected more from the chestnut. There were whisperings that the gelding was in over his head, that he had been promoted beyond his capabilities and would struggle until set some easier tasks. Millman had known it wasn't going to be easy. It wasn't.

Just over three weeks later he was back for the Group 2 Goodwood Cup and another clash with Yeats, this time over two miles. He had never had the greatest of luck at the Sussex track but Millman was relatively hamstrung regarding his options, given Sergeant Cecil's rating and his pattern of running. Taking on Yeats again was also not ideal, as not even the sunniest of optimists gave the Irish horse's rivals much of a squeak of turning the Ascot tables. Land N'Stars renewed acquaintance, as did Winged D'Argent, Golden Quest, Tungsten Strike, High Action and Balkan Knight - but as it turned out they were all playing for place money anyway, as Yeats produced a repeat of his Ascot stroll in hacking home by five lengths, smashing the track record into the bargain. Behind him were the usual Goodwood tales of woe.

Sergeant Cecil had a good position on the rail until the field swung right-handed down the hill towards home about five furlongs out, when with various parts of the rail dolled out there was certain to be trouble. "I was conscious that he'd flattened out when seeing too much daylight on an earlier run at Goodwood, so I wanted to keep him inside," says Munro. "The race didn't really take off until the top of the hill, and then I lost my position going down. Yeats had been right there in front of me, but while we were struggling to hold position he and the principals quickened away and we couldn't go with them. After that they were so far in front that it didn't matter whether I went inside or outside. I stayed on the rail, got held up again, and then he stayed on very well past beaten horses to be fourth. We would never have beaten Yeats whatever, but I think we'd have been second but for the trouble in running."

"It was a nightmare," says Millman. "It was very disappointing, but that's life. Paul Doe on Land N'Stars (sixth) said he'd never seen a horse go past him so fast, after Cecil had got going when it was all too late."

The general assessment of the race took Munro's line, as many seemed to believe that Sergeant Cecil was a 'moral' second, the five lengths he finished behind Geordieland being at least comparable to the ground he conceded through his trials and tribulations. Another point Millman raised was that the horse had hardly had a race, as he was only in top gear for around a furlong. There were silver linings to the dark cloud of defeat, but the fact remained that Sergeant Cecil had run five times in 2006 and had failed to get his head in front. It was disappointing - but what followed was worse.

# CHAPTER EIGHT

# BRINGING ON THE SUPERSUB

Two days before Sergeant Cecil returned to action, Alan Munro suffered what was described as a convulsion on a flight to Deauville, where he was to ride Dutch Art in the Group 1 Prix Morny, a race the colt subsequently won. Immediately stopped from riding until tests were carried out, Munro was later told he would have to sit out an 'observation period' of a year before being permitted to reapply for a licence.

"I was grounded because this type of blackout could be linked to epilepsy, but the test for that was clear, which was a huge relief," says Munro.

"What actually happened was that I fainted. I got up that morning and had nothing to eat, so my sugar levels would have been low. I'd just moved to a new house so there were still boxes on the stairs, and I tripped, fell and banged my head.

"I didn't think anything of it at the time and about 20 minutes later I was on the plane. My blood pressure must have been a bit low and there wasn't enough blood getting to my head, so I fainted. Fainting is one of the body's defence mechanisms, its purpose is to drop you to the floor and get blood to your head, but I was sitting upright, belted in, on the plane, so my body couldn't do that and I went into convulsion.

"I'd had a couple of convulsions in the past, both linked to a head injury, and both times I was stood down for an 'observation period'. When the year is up I'll be re-examined and retested, and hopefully get my licence back. I don't see this as the end of my career. I'd like to enjoy another five years in the saddle.

"I'll go back to Shanghai and carry on with my karate, and come back at the end of July to start the examination process."

That unexpected incident left Millman and Cooper casting around for a substitute at short notice. At that late stage it was really a question of getting the best available, and a quick scan of the entries for the Group 2 Lonsdale Cup told Millman that Frankie Dettori didn't have a ride. A phone call to Dettori's agent Ray Cochrane later, he did. "He's a fantastic jockey, everyone knows that," says Cooper, "but what interested us more was that his style of riding was similar to Alan's - both sit low in the saddle, very smooth and streamlined. We were lucky to get him at such short notice." Dettori didn't have time to travel to Kentisbeare to ride work on the horse, but he had ridden against him often enough and there was no shortage of tapes to examine. He also spoke to Munro, who passed on as much inside knowledge as he could, and to Millman, who underlined the necessity to get the horse settled in the early stages of a race.

So the public's jockey joined forces with the public's horse, who was returning to his favourite racecourse. As Cecil has matured he has become the complete professional as far as overnight trips to the races go, and there's something about York that evidently satisfies him. "He loves going overnight and he loves York," says Davey. "If you want to make him happy, just put him in a stable at York overnight. He has a nose around for five minutes and then stands in the back of his box perfectly happy. He never puts his head over the door, you'd know there was something wrong with him if he did."

The Knavesmire had dried out since the Yorkshire Cup, quicker ground not quicksand, although there was still plenty of give in it, which was a slight worry to Millman. With Yeats elsewhere, this represented an obvious chance for Sergeant Cecil to return to winning form and he was backed accordingly, going off the 11-4 favourite to beat ten rivals including the by now ubiquitous High Action, Tungsten Strike, Winged D'Argent and Golden Quest. It had taken Munro a few rides before

Frankie Dettori waves his whip in salute as Sergeant Cecil
beats Franklins Gardens in the Lonsdale Cup at York

he was secure in the knowledge that he and Sergeant Cecil were working as a team,
and for all Dettori's confidence and talent, he knew he would have to hit it off with
the horse almost immediately if he was to bring out the best in him. He settled him
down nicely at the back of the field and bided his time.

"As we turned for home I began to panic because we were too detached from the
main group," says Dettori. "It was hard to get him closer because he comes on the
bridle really quickly - once he gets going, there's no going back. So I tried to stay

patient, even though we were about ten lengths off the pace, and then I asked him to go and catch the leader. And he didn't go!"

By this time, the talented but inconsistent Franklins Gardens, evidently on a going day, was making the best of his way home and held a healthy advantage. Dettori was pushing and kicking to little avail. He says: "After a furlong I thought we'd had it, that there was too much to do, and then voom - the turbo kicked in. Looking back, Alan had warned me that he hits a flat spot before picking up properly. Then I started

The packed York stands witness Sergeant Cecil's first Group-race success

The Whistling Teal and Bulwark, left behind in the final furlong thinking that we might get there, and he was ever so good, ever so gutsy, and even pulled out a bit more in the closing stages."

He got there. Sergeant Cecil collared Franklins Gardens deep in the final furlong and outfought him after a brief duel to win by half a length. The third horse, the veteran The Whistling Teal, was five lengths back. It was his first Group-race victory. At the age of seven, he had bridged the gap from handicaps and finally made his mark against the best stayers around. A delighted Millman waxed lyrical about Dettori on Racing UK in the immediate heady aftermath, and then went down to the winner's enclosure to welcome him home. Dettori being Dettori, and Sergeant Cecil being Sergeant Cecil, the exuberant Italian thought the performance worthy of a flying dismount of the sort he usually saved for Group 1 wins, after borrowing the gymnastics from the legendary Puerto Rican rider Angel Cordero.

"It was a great relief to win that first Group race with Cecil," says Millman. "At the same time, I felt very sorry for Alan. He gave the horse the confidence to win his races, and Frankie was lucky, he got on the finished article. He said he was 'very chuffed to take the ride on the little horse trained in Devon, thank you for giving me the ride', when really it was a privilege for me to have him aboard."

He later told the *Racing Post*: "Last year was a dream and this year we've been waking up from the dream. What a horse to be involved with, and what a great ride Frankie has given him. If I could ride as well as that I would have ridden him that way. It was fantastic. It's just a shame Alan wasn't here." Dettori added: "This is for Alan. Let's hope he gets well soon as we miss him."

Cooper, an eager archivist, saves his racecards and badges as many do, although he goes a step further by being able to hang on to the sponsors' rugs that Sergeant Cecil wears after each big victory, and his sofa is currently adorned with the Weatherbys-emblazoned blanket thrown over the chestnut's back after the Lonsdale.

Alastair Down spoke of building a shrine to the horse; Cooper has all the raw materials. The pressure was off now after the unavailing struggle of the first half of the season. Cooper confesses now to his own moments of doubt regarding Sergeant Cecil's ability in the top races, but he has backed the horse to the hilt from the moment he clapped eyes on him and any fleeting misgivings were surely soon assuaged by his strong undercurrent of faith in the white-faced chestnut. "It was all starting again," he smiles.

The programme book seemed right behind Sergeant Cecil too, because nearly three weeks after the Lonsdale Cup came the Doncaster Cup. That was good, but better still was the fact that the Group 2 contest was being run at York while Doncaster underwent redevelopment. The stars were aligning in Team Cecil's favour once again.

With a Group win in the bag, the last remaining pangs of unease had been swept away, and considering that the track, trip and going were all in Sergeant Cecil's favour in the Doncaster Cup, hopes were high that he could go one better than the previous year, when he had been pounced on in the last strides by Millenary. This time there were no former Classic winners in opposition, just a handful of familiar faces who had all been comfortably vanquished on several occasions. Sergeant Cecil was the even-money favourite to see off his seven rivals - even-money to win a Group 2 race. If you had suggested that to Millman or Cooper just 18 months earlier, one of them would have kept you talking while the other ran off to summon the men in white coats. Expectation meant pressure, though - if he didn't win this Group race, people would be queuing up to undermine his ability again.

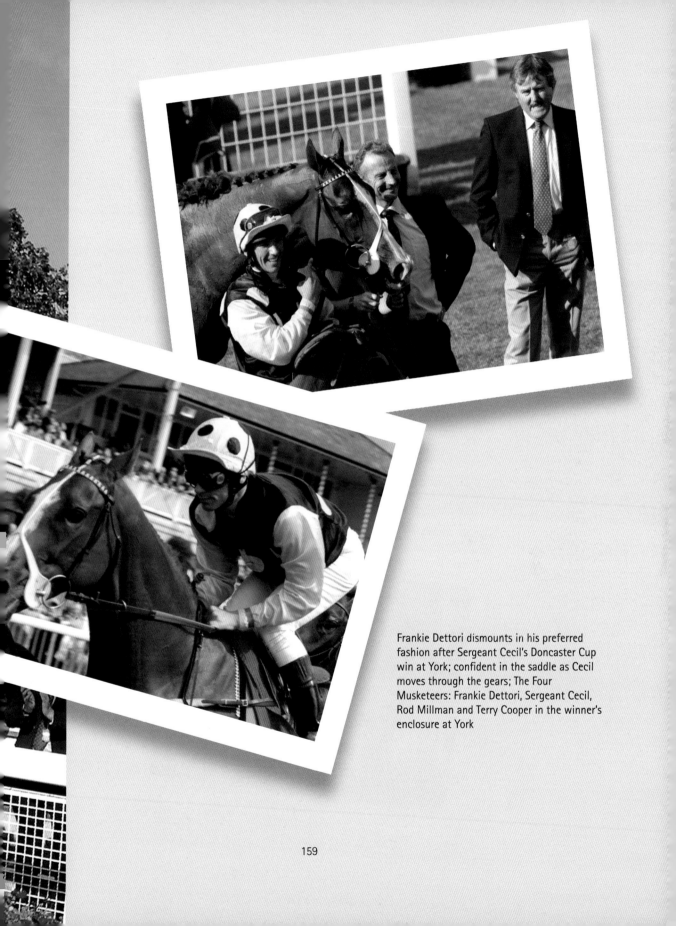

Frankie Dettori dismounts in his preferred fashion after Sergeant Cecil's Doncaster Cup win at York; confident in the saddle as Cecil moves through the gears; The Four Musketeers: Frankie Dettori, Sergeant Cecil, Rod Millman and Terry Cooper in the winner's enclosure at York

Dettori, without a ride for his retaining stable Godolphin in the race, was available to renew his acquaintance - it seemed that everything was in position for another triumph. However, as events at Sandown a couple of months earlier had shown, there was little point in counting chickens. There was still plenty that could go wrong.

With prior knowledge of Sergeant Cecil's little foibles, Dettori was more aware of what was required and settled down in second-last place as the grey Kasthari set a steady pace. The first mile was as uneventful as it gets, but what happened next had Millman spitting feathers. "It was a worrying race to watch because of Tadgh O'Shea," he says. "He was on Clara Allen, last of all, and the mare started to run a bit keen so he tried to cover her up a bit. Unfortunately, that meant running up the back of Cecil, and he clipped his heels three times. If you look at the tape you can see Frankie turning round to say something to Tadgh - I don't think he was very pleased! It would have been like Cecil getting a crack with the whip, it would have geed him up and set him off a bit too early."

Dettori dealt with the problem. He put the strong-arm on Sergeant Cecil and held him back again while the others surged forward, biding his time before lighting the blue touch-paper. "I switched him off again," he says. "I waited for him to hit his flat spot and

I thought I'd get going a bit later this time. But when I decided it was time to make up some ground, probably because he'd got himself a bit fired up, he did it in about 100 yards - we got there a furlong too soon.

"So I just thought 'oh well, we're here now, may as well keep going' and I drove him out. He drifted towards the rail but he had plenty left in the tank."

Sergeant Cecil ranged up alongside the 11-year-old Alcazar well over a furlong out, poked his nose in front and immediately started to edge towards the stands' rail. There was clear daylight to make the manoeuvre, but in the process Alcazar got an accidental rap over the nose from Dettori's whip. Alcazar was switched and kept on gamely but never had a hope of catching Sergeant Cecil, who bounded across the line a length clear. The stewards held an inquiry, but soon came to the conclusion that nothing had happened to influence the outcome of the race and allowed the result to stand.

The race summarisers on Racing UK christened him the 'greatest sergeant since Bilko', and Dettori played to the gallery with another flying dismount in the winner's enclosure. Millman was more concerned about the damage to Cecil's hind legs, which had received a good clattering from the hooves of Clara Allen. "He basically came within a fraction of breaking down," he says. "If any of those cuts had been any deeper they would have damaged his tendon - as it was they got infected and it was quite nasty for a time. It's the kind of thing I would have expected to happen in the Cesarewitch with 30 runners around him, but not in an eight-runner Group race with plenty of room for everyone."

Dettori had a word with Cooper and Millman after the race. "Frankie said that we ought to send him to France for the Prix du Cadran," says Cooper. "Rod said 'do you think he's up to that?' and Frankie just nodded. Rod said 'if we do, will you ride him?', and Frankie grinned and said 'no problem.'"

## Fanfare for the uncommon horse

It wasn't exactly Operation Overlord, but the decision to go for the Group 1 Prix du Cadran, at Longchamp on Prix de l'Arc de Triomphe day, was a bold one, although frankly Sergeant Cecil had nothing to lose and plenty to gain. Yeats wouldn't be waiting for him in the Bois de Boulogne, as he was already in Australia being prepared for the Melbourne Cup, and there was no other stayer in Europe to whom Sergeant Cecil needed to doff his cap.

There were few targets in Britain left for the chestnut, save for the Jockey Club Cup and Millman had the progressive Hawridge Prince earmarked for that, so it made perfect sense to send Sergeant Cecil overseas for a race that was likely to suit him very well. France was his destination, just as it had been for his namesake almost 100 years earlier. First things first, however, as Davey had to equip herself with a passport. Having never previously been abroad, Davey had been known around The Paddocks as 'Sue with no passport' which, although an unwieldy nickname, seemed to sum things up neatly on that front. She's probably just known as 'Sue' now.

With her documentation intact, Davey, Jack Micklem and Sergeant Cecil set off on the ferry for France on the Friday before Sunday's race, all the transport requirements having been overseen by Alan Walters, a friend of Millman's. "I was more worried about the journey than the horse," says Davey. "He took the crossing and all the palaver as though he'd been doing it all his life, he just loves the travelling."

Since the French-bred Gladiateur

(although trained by the Newmarket-based Tom Jennings) won the Triple Crown in 1865 and gained the nickname 'The Avenger of Waterloo', the rivalry on the racecourse between Britain and France has mirrored that of the population of each country. Top-class stayers such as four-time Cadran hero Marsyas and the mighty Sagaro, triple winner of the Ascot Gold Cup, have plied their trade successfully in Britain, while on almost every weekend of the Flat season British horses travel over to take on the French in their own back yard in races great and small.

Arc weekend always sees a huge exodus of horses and people across the Channel, and Sergeant Cecil was joined in the Cadran by Alcazar and Baddam, who had filled the minor placings in the Doncaster Cup. There were only seven runners in all - the three British raiders, the German gelding Le Miracle, and three local hopes led by the familiar Reefscape and backed up by Shamdala and Petite Speciale. There was no-one to fear - at his best Sergeant Cecil was more than a match for all six. The two and a half miles around leafy Longchamp wouldn't be a problem, especially considering the gentle amble that characterises the early stages of every French race, and the ground was good.

Millman wanted to go there and back in a day, so Cooper splashed out and hired a light aircraft for six - Terry and Sue, Rod and Louise, Neville and Terry's son Ian. The airborne division left Hurn airfield early and was in Paris little more than an hour later. Taxis to the racecourse followed. Millman hadn't had many runners abroad and had never been to Longchamp, so on arrival it took quite some time to locate Sergeant Cecil. When he was found, he took Cooper's breath away. "As soon as I saw him, I thought 'yes, you're up for it today'," he says. "It was the best I've seen him look - he had a glint in his eye that made him look like he meant business, which was very encouraging. Apparently he'd been quiet the previous day but had revved himself up on Sunday, coming to the boil at the right time."

The morning flew past. The Cadran was the first race on the card, and Team Cecil barely had time to become overawed by the occasion or carried away on wings of overconfidence as the decisive hour approached. One man who made light of the situation was Dettori, who was on top form. Cooper says: "Frankie was full of himself, he was so funny and had us all in fits of laughter. We had a bottle of champagne before the race, and then it was time to find a vantage point from which to watch the action."

Davey says: "There was an electric atmosphere before the race, it was incredible. Frankie got the leg-up and I led Cecil out to the track, let him go, and he lobbed off down to the start like an old gent. I watched him go, and then I found a spot on the fence by the winning post to watch the race and to be close when it came to leading him in."

Millman did the customary interviews with the media scrum (in English) and then climbed up into the stands, where he had a nasty shock awaiting him. "I found a good place to watch from, and then I looked down and there was a cameraman in front of me," he says. "He said he'd been told to keep the camera on me to pick up my reaction during the race - it's lucky he hadn't turned his camera on early, as he'd have picked up another kind of reaction entirely."

Cooper likes to watch Sergeant Cecil's races on his own. Sometimes tension is easier to deal with alone rather than in a group. The others melted into grandstands already packed to overflowing with British invaders, most with a bottle or two inside them and euros both in their pockets and on the white nose of Sergeant Cecil, and ready to get the meeting off to a good start by roaring home their old favourite. There was nothing left to do but watch and hope.

It was in Dettori's hands now. He knew the intricacies of the track and had just one thing in mind - switch the horse off and settle him down in last place. "There was

a huge British crowd that day and they cheered him all the way to the start," he says.
"That got him on his toes a bit and I knew it would be important to relax him."
Sergeant Cecil broke well and Dettori restrained him towards the back of the field. Only
Baddam was behind him as Le Miracle and Shamdala set the pace, and Sergeant Cecil
was relaxed and conserving energy. As the field passed the stands for the first time a
great shout went up.

"Baddam was leaning on Frankie as they turned away from the stands,
intimidating him and buzzing him along a little bit," says Millman. "Frankie did the
right thing by pulling him back behind Baddam, and he soon relaxed again. The race
seemed to go on forever."

Sergeant Cecil brought up the rear for the next mile. "He was very relaxed at the
back and I was happy," says Dettori, "but then the tempo quickened and the leaders
started to get away a little bit." The move had also been noted by Cooper, who says:
"They hadn't gone that quick, they never do in France, and he seemed to drop off them
a little bit. Then it took half a furlong to wake him up. I wasn't too worried, though, I
knew he had gears."

So did Dettori. "I didn't panic - I knew he had a tremendous turn of foot for a
stayer. I had no doubt he'd pick them up as long as no-one got in his way."

There are two straights at Longchamp - the false straight leads to the real one. The
false straight is the tomb of false hopes; every jockey knows to wait until the final
bend before committing all in a dash for glory. Dettori waited. Baddam moved away
from the rail and Sergeant Cecil mirrored the move. A gap appeared between Petite
Speciale and Alcazar and Dettori arrowed the gelding through it into fourth place.
Sergeant Cecil loved to drive between horses; it stirred his blood and turned him into
the warrior after whom he was named. Down he came upon them like a wolf
upon the fold.

Frankie Dettori and Sergeant Cecil sweep past Le Miracle
(rails) and Shamdala to clinch the Cadran

Millman, watching under the steady gaze of television viewers around the world, leaned his head forward to better see the *denouement*. "He got past a couple, and then Frankie pushed the button. I thought 'oh good, he's going to be third, a good effort in a Group 1' and a second later he was off - oh, he won easy."

"It took him a furlong to get going, and then he went," says Dettori. "It was like firing a bullet."

A furlong out, Sergeant Cecil had three lengths to make up. And, just like that, he did. Va-va-voom.

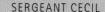

Frankie Dettori makes his point to the crowd at Longchamp after Sergeant Cecil's Prix du Cadran victory

The speed passed on by King's Signet all those years ago came bubbling out in one glorious torrent as Sergeant Cecil devoured the gap between himself and the leaders. After almost two and a half miles, he summoned up a burst of acceleration that would not have been out of place in the Arc itself and went past Le Miracle and Shamdala as though they were standing still. They may as well have been. Dettori turned his head towards them as he swept by, his mouth wide in a shout of triumph and wonder as he eased back down through the gears in the last 50 yards, his arm raised in acclamation as they crossed the line three-quarters of a length to the good.

And then it was simply so much pandemonium. The last furlong and a half had been played out to the backdrop of a wall of sound that would have done Phil Spector credit, as the battalions of Brits threw back their heads and howled Sergeant Cecil home. Dettori felt the roar hit him even in the heat of battle - "I could hear it following me as I came up the straight, it was like the Doppler effect of an aeroplane going past" - and knew there was plenty left where that came from. Racing's greatest showman knew how to milk an appreciative crowd, and he held Sergeant Cecil back long after his rivals had left the course to maximise the effect of parading him in front of the stands. "It was like I'd won the Arc," he says.

As Davey took Sergeant Cecil up the walkway back to the winner's enclosure, Millman caught up with them. "A lot of our owners had gone over for the race, and as I was walking back with Cecil I could hear them shouting our names, I could see them waving and reaching out to us. It was like the Cheltenham Festival after an Irish-trained favourite has won," he says.

"Louise caught up with me halfway down the walkway, she was quite emotional, and we walked in with him together. It was almost too much -  it was my first Group 1 win and what a way to do it."

Terry and Sue Cooper were also dealing with the emotion of the moment. "The fanfare as he walked back through the crowds was unbelievable," says Terry. "I was dumbfounded, I didn't know whether to laugh or cry. People lined the rails six or seven deep to welcome him back, cheering and shouting, and he hardly turned a hair. It sounds silly, but I found it hard to realise that it was actually my horse they were cheering - I found myself saying 'Cooper, that's your little boy there'. Incredible."

Dettori jumped off in his customary manner and the crowd cheered again, and kept cheering. They didn't stop until Davey led Sergeant Cecil away.

Dettori told the *Racing Post*: "Did you hear the roar out there? I thought it was going to be tight and then he suddenly picked up. It's a great start for the Brits and they were all on. I could hear them all roaring for 'The Sergeant' and it felt like they were all pushing me on. I've never known anything like it, and I think he heard the crowd too. What a horse. What a story."

The only man missing was the one who had done so much to fashion Cecil into the finished article. Alan Munro didn't even see the Cadran because he had no access to live pictures at his home, but later told the *Post*'s Graham Dench: "I think it's brilliant that the horse has reached such a peak and won a Group 1, and I'm really pleased for everyone - the owners, Rod of course, and the horse himself. I'm pleased for Frankie too, and I'll give him a big hug when I see him. I think I was fortunate to get on him at the right time. He started to progress and has never stopped. He's a superstar." Millman later said: "Alan gave the horse the confidence to show his full ability after he'd been partnered by a lot of different jockeys. It's such a shame Alan's not here, but if it's up to me he'll be his ride again if he comes back."

"Then we went for a couple more bottles of champagne," smiles Cooper. "We bumped into Alastair Down and, knowing he was such a big fan of the horse, invited him along too. We all sat round a table soaking up the atmosphere - it was a wonderful climax to the day."

Down paid tribute to the horse in his next *Post* column, writing: "If the Arc result was somehow unsatisfactory for headline-writers, the so-called undercard was rich indeed. I carry a bit of a torch for Sergeant Cecil, and after the old trouper had won the Prix du Cadran, owner Terry Cooper and trainer Rod Millman asked me up to share a bottle of champagne or two. Sat round the table were the most down-to-earth bunch of west country men and women you could ever ask to meet. Most of us involved with a horse as remarkable as the Sergeant would acquire some shocking airs and graces. Not this lot.

"This old stayer has taken them to places undreamed of by even the most fanciful of owners, yet not a moment of that spectacular odyssey has been lost on them. On that journey the racing public has become deeply involved and intertwined with a horse for whom their affection is thumpingly genuine.

"The reception he received on Sunday was genuinely moving and even Frankie Dettori, no stranger to moments of magic, understood that he was playing a major role in the most special of productions.

"Between us all, we made Sergeant Cecil 'Horse of the Year' in 2005, a wonderful achievement for an animal who some dismissed as a mere handicapper. Now the mere handicapper is a Group 1 winner, and the nicest thing about it is that neither owner nor trainer think they are in any way more important than they were a year ago.

"Success is a wonderful thing. Success that doesn't go to your head is a rarity."

The happy band left before the last – "My only regret was that we didn't go out on the town and celebrate," says Millman - and spent a sweet hour in the airport reception area, drinking more champagne and sharing it with no less a celebrity than Aidan O'Brien, who had beaten them twice that year with Yeats and, while waiting for his flight back to Ballydoyle, had wandered over to offer his congratulations on their first Group 1 success.

The flight back was just as memorable as the rest of the day - the little plane was flung around like thistledown by bad weather on the approach to Hurn, leading more than one of the party to mouth the words 'never again' on reaching the safety of the runway - and then it was all back to chez Cooper, where Don Hazzard and his son Clive were later to join them for champagne, a chinese takeaway and repeated reviews of the Cadran tape.

"What happened was a miracle," says Cooper. "And for him to be named after father makes you think that there is divine intervention, a little bit of help from above at the right time." Old soldiers never die; their names live on forever.

# CHAPTER NINE

# NOW ALL WE HAVE TO DO IS
# DO IT ALL OVER AGAIN

The year wasn't over for Sergeant Cecil, although perhaps for the sake of neatness, of tying up the ends to form a satisfying whole, it should have been. Three weeks after the Cadran came the Group 1 Prix Royal-Oak over just short of two miles, the French equivalent of the St Leger but open to older horses. A Classic by name if not by nature, it offered another opportunity for Sergeant Cecil to pick up a valuable prize and more prestige, as well as to further delight his army of adoring fans.

Back they all went to Longchamp, all except for Frankie Dettori, who was required to ride in Italy for Godolphin. Another supersub was sought and found, this time in the shape of new British champion Ryan Moore, a rider who had taken the season by the scruff of the neck at the tender age of 23. Moore, instilled with the requisite knowledge to enable him to perform the 'Sergeant Cecil ride', rode a very similar race to the one Dettori constructed in the Cadran, but no two races are alike and this time Sergeant Cecil was destined to play only a supporting role.

Millman says: "Ryan rode basically the same race that Frankie had, and he beat both the horses from the Cadran that also ran in the Royal-Oak, but this time he didn't win. It was just one of those things. The gaps didn't open for him and he was left a little flat-footed when the pace suddenly quickened."

Moore did a fine job in settling him in the early stages, but was further out of his ground than was Dettori and, when the front-runners suddenly quickened off what had been no more than a steady pace, found himself with a lot to do. He got Sergeant

Cecil running in the last furlong and was finishing best of all, but the leaders had flown and he went under by just over a length behind Montare. The *Racing Post* race analyst wrote: "With his style of running, there is always a danger of that [getting going too late] happening and it would be no surprise to see him turn the tables on the two horses that beat him here should they clash again next season."

Cooper thinks the horse should have won, but is equally swift to concede that Sergeant Cecil was coming to the end of a long season, and that the dizzying rush that Dettori elicited from him in the closing stages of the Cadran may have taxed his stout constitution more than was realised. It was not the way to end, but at least Sergeant Cecil had been placed in a Classic - surely the expectation furthest from

Cecil works off a spot of excess energy at Paradise Farm Stud under the watchful eye of Terry Cooper

'Sergeant Cecil'

CECIL EDWARD
COOPER
DIED 6TH MARCH 1956
AGED 59.
MUCH LOVED
HUSBAND AND FATHER.
'WE KNOW
YOU·ARE·ALWAYS·WITH·US,
THANKS·FOR·ALL·YOUR·HELP.'

Cooper's mind when he phoned the vet six years earlier and asked him to come over to make a gelding of his colt.

They packed up the pieces and went home. Sergeant Cecil went back to Paradise Farm Stud, where as far as Neville Poole is concerned there will be a box and a paddock for as long as he wants. The *Racing Post*/ROA awards came and went without Sergeant Cecil being honoured a second time, even after Paul Haigh stated his case eloquently in the *Post*, ending thus: "Sergeant Cecil is brave, tough, game, honest, trustworthy, and, it seems, increasingly enthusiastic. Never mind Horse of the Year. I want him for leader of the Labour Party." The outstanding mare Ouija Board ran off with all the awards going, although Sergeant Cecil did pick up the trophy for the racing category in the annual Animal Health Trust UK equestrian awards, another gong voted for by readers of the *Racing Post*.

Don Hazzard also gained recognition from *Thoroughbred Owner & Breeder* magazine, which presented him with the Small Breeder Special Merit award for October and November following Sergeant Cecil's Cadran victory. Hazzard had had a lucrative summer, taking home valuable breeders' prizes after the Lonsdale and Doncaster Cups, and although the French race offered no such prize for British breeders, Cooper dipped into his own pocket and 'saw him right' at Hazzard's 80th birthday party in December. Team Cecil was one big family and no-one ever got left out.

Over the winter, Cooper did something he'd been meaning to do for 50 years. Sergeant Cecil the horse had been named after Cooper's late father, a flesh-and-blood memorial in place of the headstone that money couldn't be made to stretch to in the straitened circumstances after his death. Now the old soldier has two memorials.

"We thought that we would never bother with a headstone, because the horse has been so much better," says Cooper. "But after a bit of thought I changed my

The headstone for the first Sergeant Cecil – Terry Cooper's father

mind, and we had a stone placed. I'm very glad we did - it made it a bigger thing, more than just a piece of ground. It made it a fitting thing.

"I don't know whether my father liked racing, but it's lovely that the name Sergeant Cecil is now known all over the world. I mean, what are the chances of giving a name that means so much to me to a horse who has gone on to do what he's done? Fifty million to one? It's just out of this world."

As 2007 began, Millman welcomed Sergeant Cecil back from Paradise - Cooper says: "It's relaxing to get him back to Rod's. He's a once-in-a-lifetime horse, so I worry about him when he's here. It's a bit sad not seeing him at 3pm every day, but it's also a relief when the pressure's off and he's back in training" - and began to consider what the next season might bring. Yeats would be back for more, although the likes of Franklins Gardens, Reefscape and Alcazar had earned themselves a luxurious retirement. As Sergeant Cecil settled back into box no.2, between Masai Moon and Mustajed, from where he can stare amiably into the Millmans' bedroom, his trainer was busy concocting plans of world domination for the eight-year-old.

"Now all we have to do is do it all over again!" he says. "This year I think we'll definitely go for a couple of the bigger mile-and-a-half races, although I'm not saying we'd pass up the chance to run over two miles if the right race was there at the right time.

"I don't think he'll ever go for the Melbourne Cup, though, not many horses go down there and pick up where they left off when they come back. It takes a big chunk out of a horse's career. But I would like to take him abroad to chase some big prize-money, so I'll think about Japan and Hong Kong, if we get an invitation or two.

"And I'm not ruling out the King George, either, depending on the field. It would be a brave man who would say for certain that he wouldn't have been placed in the race last year - there were only six runners, and I've nothing against Enforcer (fourth) but I wouldn't be afraid of taking him on - and Terry was a bit put out that I didn't enter him, although the entry fees are very high.

"He'll probably start off like he did last year, in the John Porter, then the Yorkshire Cup, and then the Ascot Gold Cup. Then maybe back to Ascot for the King George, because if we did miss one of the staying races it would be the Goodwood Cup, as the track has never really suited him, although if there was a small field you never know. Then back to York for the Lonsdale, then the Doncaster Cup, then the Cadran, then a little bit of globe-trotting, hopefully."

Cooper is looking forward to it, although he is also well aware that at some point the sands of time will start to run away and the years will begin to hang heavy on Sergeant Cecil's legs. "Hopefully we'll have at least another year, but whatever happens Cecil won't be allowed to go downhill," he says. "As soon as I think he's gone off the top he won't go any further, he deserves better than to keep going round the tracks when he can't do what he did before.

"I don't know what we'll do with him when the time comes for retirement. Obviously he'll never be sold or given away, but he would need to be kept active and interested. Somebody from the National Stud once told me that Cecil would be very welcome there as a visitor attraction for a few months a year, and that sounds the sort of thing he'd like."

Until that day comes, Millman will send Sergeant Cecil far and wide in search of greater glories, while Sharon Steel keeps him

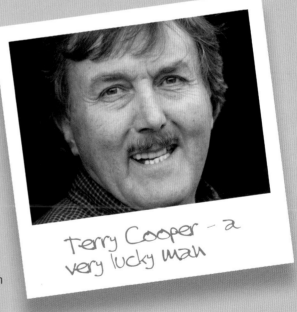

Terry Cooper - a very lucky man

happy on the gallops and Sue Davey attends to his every need in the stable, both prompt with the carrots and mints when required. There is more than a spot of hero-worship involved here, but only on a private level - you would never get them to shout from the rooftops about him. They both say: "He's just Cecil - it's very hard to put into words what he means to us. He's so brave and gutsy and never lets us down. He's special but he's just our boy."

That goes for the racing public too. Few horses insinuate themselves into the fabric of the sport as has Sergeant Cecil. There is something about the horse that appeals across the whole spectrum of racing, from professionals to punters, from the seen-it-all hacks to the bright-eyed enthusiasts, and few of them could pinpoint what it was about him that drew from them such affection. Although all over the world, in every culture, there is a particular delight in and reverence for the story of a hardworking boy from a humble background, who pays his dues, overcomes many obstacles and rises, through his own ability and tenacity, to achieve glory, or attain power, or to simply realise his dreams and the dreams of those closest to him.

Does it sound familiar?

RACING RECORD

# Sergeant Cecil
## chestnut gelding, 2-5-1999

| | | | |
|---|---|---|---|
| | | | Nearctic |
| | | Northern Dancer | |
| | Nureyev | | Natalma |
| | | | Forli |
| | | Special | |
| King's Signet Ch 1989 | | | Thong |
| | | | Sir Gaylord |
| | | Habitat | |
| | Sigy | | Little Hut |
| | | | Primera |
| | | Satu | |
| | | | Creation |
| | | | Hail To Reason |
| | | Roberto | |
| | Touching Wood | | Bramalea |
| | | | Vaguely Noble |
| | | Mandera | |
| Jadidh B 1988 | | | Foolish One |
| | | | Petingo |
| | | Troy | |
| | Petrol | | La Milo |
| | | | Silly Season |
| | | Rambling Rose | |
| | | | Honeysuckle Rose |

*Bred by Don Hazzard in Britain*

## Sire **King's Signet**

Unraced at 2, won 2 (both 6f) of 6 starts at 3, won 3 (inc. Stewards' Cup, Listed Scarbrough S) of 6 starts at 4. Progressed into very useful sprinter, though well beaten only 2 starts in Pattern company. By top-class miler and outstanding sire of variety of performers, mainly milers and sprinters. Half-brother to Gr3 winners Radjhasi and Sicyos out of outstanding sprinter. First foals 1995, exported after 2000 covering season to Saudi Arabia. Very modest record overall from limited chances, sire of: Bali Royal (Listed winner), Sergeant Cecil (Gr1 winner).

## Dam **Jadidh**

Unraced at 2, placed over 14f only Flat start at 3. Placed over 2m1f in 8 subsequent Flat starts. Won 6 (2m1f to 2m6f) of 57 starts over hurdles from 3 to 9. By St Leger winner with poor stud record. Half-sister to Listed winner Refuse To Lose. Dam half-sister to useful 2yo Rahik (grand-dam of Gr3-winning 2yo Kings Point) out of smart sprinter Rambling Rose. Dam of: Sergeant Cecil (1999 g by King's Signet; Gr1 winner), Jayer Gilles (2000 g by Busy Flight; placed), 2003 c by Kayf Tara.

## Assessment

Sergeant Cecil has outrun his pedigree in terms of both stamina and class. Although his dam was a hurdler by a St Leger winner, she is from a fairly pacy family, and speed underpins King's Signet's performance and pedigree. It is tempting to attribute Sergeant Cecil's stamina to maternal grandsire Touching Wood, but in the end the gelding is one of those Flat horses best judged without reference to his pedigree.

**Trainer: B R Millman   Owner: Terry Cooper**
**Breeder: D E Hazzard**
**King's Signet (USA) (7.1f) – Jadidh (Touching Wood (USA) (12.4f)**
**first foal: dam, placed at 14f/17f on Flat and winning hurdler, half-sister to 9f Listed winner Refuse To Lose**

| RACE TYPE | STARTS | WINS | 2nds | 3rds | WIN PRIZE | TOTAL PRIZE | BEST TS | BEST RPR | BHB RATING |
|---|---|---|---|---|---|---|---|---|---|
| Lifetime Flat Turf | 43 | 9 | 14 | 6 | £561,487 | £726,531 | 108 | 120 | 115 |
| Lifetime All Weather | 1 | 0 | 0 | 0 | £0 | £0 | 59 | 66 | 65 |
| Lifetime Hurdle | 0 | 0 | 0 | 0 | £0 | £0 | | | |
| Lifetime Chase | 0 | 0 | 0 | 0 | £0 | £0 | | | |
| **Lifetime All** | **44** | **9** | **14** | **6** | **£561,487** | **£726,531 (to end 2006 Flat season)** | | | |

| DATE | | RACE CONDITIONS | | WGT | RACE OUTCOME | | JOCKEY | OR | TS | RPR |
|---|---|---|---|---|---|---|---|---|---|---|
| 22 Oct 06 | Lon | 16Gd | | G1,98K | 9-4 | 3/10 | 1¼L, Montare[27/10] 9-1 | Ryan Moore | – | 79 | 117 |
| 1 Oct 06 | Lon | 20Gd | | G1,98K | 9-2 | 1/7 | ¾L, Shamdala[2/1F] 8-13 | L Dettori | – | 65 | 120 |
| 8 Sep 06 | Yor | 18Gd | Cl1 | G2,56K | 9-4 | 1/8 | 1L, Alcazar[EvensF] 9-1 | L Dettori | 111 | – | 118 |
| 22 Aug 06 | Yor | 16GS | Cl1 | G2,70K | 9-1 | 1/11 | ½L, Franklins Gardens[11/4F] 9-1 | L Dettori | 111 | 102 | 117 |
| 3 Aug 06 | Goo | 16GF | Cl1 | G2,56K | 9-5 | 4/15 | 10L, Yeats[10/1] 9-10 | Alan Munro | 110 | 89 | 109 |
| 8 Jul 06 | San | 16GF | Cl1 | L,15K | 9-0 | 2/5 | ¼L, Land 'n Stars[5/6F] 9-3 | Alan Munro | 111 | 43 | 106 |
| 22 Jun 06 | Asc | 20GF | Cl1 | G1,136K | 9-2 | 5/12 | 8¾L, Yeats[5/1] 9-2 | Alan Munro | 111 | 100 | 112 |
| 19 May 06 | Yor | 14Sft | Cl1 | G2,79K | 8-12 | 2/7 | 3L, Percussionist[9/2] 8-12 | Alan Munro | 112 | 46 | 113 |
| 22 Apr 06 | Nby | 12Gd | Cl1 | G3,28K | 8-12 | 4/11 | 3¼L, Mubtaker[9/1] 9-1 | Alan Munro | 112 | 80 | 111 |
| 15 Oct 05 | Nmk | 18GS | Cl2 | Hc,75K | 9-8 | 1/34 | ¾L, King Revo[10/1] 8-3 | Alan Munro | 104 | 108 | 116 |
| 8 Sep 05 | Don | 18Gd | Cl1 | G2,58K | 9-1 | 2/7 | ¾L, Millenary[6/1] 9-4 | Alan Munro | 104 | 68 | 115 |
| 17 Aug 05 | Yor | 14Gd | Cl2 | Hc,130K | 8-12 | 1/20 | 1L, Carte Diamond[11/1] 9-7 | Alan Munro | 96 | 89 | 109 |
| 26 Jul 05 | Goo | 14GS | Cl2 | Hc,15K | 9-11 | 3/13 | 1¼L, Golden Quest[8/1] 10-0 | Alan Munro | 96 | 98 | 109 |
| 25 Jun 05 | Ncs | 16Gd | Cl2 | Hc,104K | 8-8 | 1/20 | 1½L, Tungsten Strike[14/1] 9-1 | Alan Munro | 92 | 56 | 102 |
| 4 Jun 05 | Eps | 12Gd | Cl2 | Hc,23K | 9-0 | 3/20 | 2½L, Crow Wood[12/1] 8-10 | Alan Munro | 92 | 100 | 102 |
| 14 May 05 | Nby | 12Fm | Cl2 | Hc,13K | 9-0 | 2/10 | 3L, Flamboyant Lad[8/1] 8-12 | Alan Munro | 92 | 48 | 98 |
| 20 Apr 05 | Eps | 12GS | Cl3 | Hc,12K | 9-5 | 12/13 | 27L, Tender Falcon[8/1] 8-7 | Alan Munro | 94 | 40 | 66 |
| 26 Sep 04 | Asc | 12GF | Cl2 | Hc,34K | 9-1 | 3/14 | 5½L, Fort[11/2] 7-13 | Jimmy Fortune | 93 | 87 | 102 |
| 10 Sep 04 | Don | 15GF | Cl2 | Hc,23K | 8-12 | 2/15 | 1¼L, Lost Soldier Three[5/1] 8-1 | Jimmy Fortune | 93 | 64 | 100 |
| 4 Sep 04 | Hay | 14Gd | Cl2 | Hc,52K | 8-12 | 2/20 | ¾L, Defining[10/1] 9-3 | Steve Drowne | 93 | 48 | 102 |
| 27 Jul 04 | Goo | 14Gd | Cl2 | Hc,29K | 9-1 | 2/15 | ½L, Mephisto[16/1] 9-4 | Jimmy Fortune | 89 | 101 | 99 |
| 9 Jul 04 | Asc | 12Gd | Cl3 | Hc,9K | 9-13 | 1/11 | shd, Cutting Crew[16/1] 9-4 | Jimmy Fortune | 86 | 83 | 95 |
| 2 Jul 04 | San | 14GS | Cl3 | Hc,9K | 9-11 | 5/7 | 17L, Quedex[4/1] 8-0 | K Fallon | 86 | 65 | 77 |
| 18 Jun 04 | Goo | 12GF | Cl4 | Hc,6K | 10-0 | 3/11 | 2L, Wait For The Will[33/1] 9-6 | Steve Drowne | 85 | 81 | 92 |
| 21 Apr 04 | Eps | 12Sft | Cl3 | Hc,15K | 9-8 | 20/20 | 98+L, Cold Turkey[20/1] 8-12 | Richard Hughes | 88 | – | – |
| 6 Sep 03 | Hay | 14GF | Cl3 | Hc,32K | 9-13 | 17/19 | 47L, The Persuader[10/1] 8-2 | Richard Hughes | 89 | – | 39 |
| 9 Aug 03 | Asc | 12GF | Cl2 | Hc,20K | 8-10 | 2/10 | ¾L, Capitano Corelli[8/1] 8-11 | K Fallon | 87 | 73 | 94 |
| 12 Jul 03 | Asc | 16GF | Cl2 | Hc,37K | 8-10 | 8/13 | 8½L, Mana D'Argent[10/1] 8-7 | Richard Hughes | 87 | – | 87 |
| 4 Jul 03 | San | 14Gd | Cl3 | Hc,9K | 9-7 | 1/10 | ¾L, Mr Ed[4/1J] 9-0 | Richard Hughes | 82 | – | 93 |
| 14 Jun 03 | San | 14GF | Cl4 | Hc,5K | 9-13 | 2/12 | 1L, Sindapour[7/1] 9-1 | Jimmy Fortune | 79 | 49 | 88 |
| 27 May 03 | San | 14GF | Cl4 | Hc,5K | 9-7 | 1/10 | 1¼L, Reveillez[12/1] 9-11 | Richard Hughes | 76 | – | 87 |
| 16 Apr 03 | Nmk | 12GF | Cl3 | Hc,9K | 8-6 | 10/11 | 20L, Chai Walla[4/1] 9-7 p | Darryll Holland | 73 | 31 | 52 |
| 7 Apr 03 | Wdr | 12GF | Cl4 | Hc,5K | 9-2 | 2/14 | shd, Palamedes[9/2J] 9-5 | Darryll Holland | 73 | 76 | 83 |
| 28 Oct 02 | Wdr | 12GS | Cl4 | 3yHc,5K | 8-12 | 2/17 | 1½L, Mystic Mile[4/1F] 9-7 | W Woods | 71 | 41 | 79 |
| 16 Oct 02 | Bat | 12Gd | Cl4 | Hc,4K | 9-0 | 2/18 | hd, Red Wine[11/2F] 9-8 | Richard Hughes | 68 | 72 | 79 |

| 2 Oct 02 | Sal | 14GS | Cl5 | Hc,3K | 9-6 | 2/14 | ¼L, Bobsleigh[6/1] 9-10 | W Woods | 65 | 47 | 75 |
| 18 Sep 02 | Bev | 12GF | Cl5 | 3yHc,5K | 9-1 | 3/14 | 1¾L, Michaels Dream[7/1] 8-1 | W Woods | 64 | 50 | 71 |
| 26 Aug 02 | Chp | 10Gd | Cl5 | Hc,3K | 9-8 | 2/16 | 3L, Lara Falana[10/1] 9-7 | Pat Eddery | 63 | 59 | 69 |
| 15 Jun 02 | San | 14Gd | Cl4 | Hc,4K | 7-5 | 6/8 | 4L, Classic Millennium[33/1] 7-4 | Francis Ferris | 65 | — | 69 |
| 16 May 02 | Sal | 12Gd | Cl4 | Hc,4K | 8-2 | 9/19 | 12½L, Showpiece[33/1] 9-0 | Martin Dwyer | 70 | 46 | 62 |
| 5 May 02 | Sal | 12GF | Cl4 | 3yMd,4K | 9-0 | 10/17 | 12½L, Gulf[66/1] 9-0 | S Righton | 70 | 35 | 64 |
| 27 Mar 02 | Lin | 10St | Cl4 | Md,2K | 8-5 | 9/14 | 6¼L, Charlie Simmons[25/1] 9-11 | S Righton | — | 59 | 66 |
| 1 Oct 01 | Bat | 10Gd | Cl4 | 2yMd,3K | 9-0 | 7/14 | 11L, Stage By Stage[100/1] 9-0 | S Righton | — | — | 69 |
| 24 Sep 01 | Kem | 8GF | Cl4 | 2yMd,4K | 9-0 | 8/11 | 11½L, Mananan McLir[100/1] 9-0 | S Righton | — | 29 | |

# KEMPTON

### 24 September 2001

Good To Firm

## 2:30  New Renault Trafic EBF Maiden Stakes (Class D) (Div I) (Class 4) (2yo) 1m

[off 2:32]     £4,465.50, £1,374.00, £687.00, £343.50

| | | | Draw | TRAINER | Age | Wgt | JOCKEY | SP | OR | TS | RPR |
|---|---|---|---|---|---|---|---|---|---|---|---|
| 1 | | Mananan McLir (USA) | 11 | J H M Gosden | 2 | 9-0 v1 | Jimmy Fortune | 6/1 | 82 | 64 | 88 |
| 2 | 1¼ | Ezz Elkheil (GB) | 2 | J W Payne | 2 | 9-0 | Jamie Spencer | 6/1 | | 60 | 85 |
| 3 | 1¼ | Shafeeq (FR) | 6 | A C Stewart | 2 | 9-0 | R Hills | 10/11F | | 56 | 82 |
| 4 | hd | No Question (GB) | 1 | B W Hills | 2 | 8-9 | Michael Hills | 8/1 | | 51 | 77 |
| 5 | 5 | Mad Carew (USA) | 5 | P W Harris | 2 | 9-0 | T Quinn | 8/1 | | 41 | 70 |
| 6 | 1¼ | Sainte Just (IRE) | 4 | R Charlton | 2 | 9-0 | Richard Hughes | 10/1 | | 37 | 67 |
| 7 | 2 | Top Prize (USA) | 3 | B J Meehan | 2 | 9-0 | Pat Eddery | 5/1 | | 31 | 63 |
| 8 | ½ | Sergeant Cecil (GB) | 8 | J W Mullins | 2 | 9-0 | S Righton | 100/1 | | 29 | 62 |
| 9 | 1¼ | Sorbonne | 10 | B Hanbury | 2 | 9-0 t | G Carter | 16/1 | | 25 | 59 |
| 10 | ½ | Treasure Trail | 9 | S Kirk | 2 | 9-0 | Dane O'Neill | 33/1 | | 23 | 58 |
| 11 | dist | Mr Ricciolo (IRE) | 7 | B J Curley | 2 | 9-0 | Ted Durcan | 33/1 | | — | |

**11 ran** TIME 1m 39.46s (slow by 0.46s)     **TOTAL SP** 141%

# BATH

### 1 October 2001

Good

## 3:00 Manny Bernstein Tax Free Debit Card EBF Maiden Stakes (Class D) (Class 4) (2yo) (1m2f46y) 1m2f

[off 3:01]     £3,513.25, £1,081.00, £540.50, £270.25

| | | | Draw | TRAINER | Age | Wgt | JOCKEY | SP | OR | TS | RPR |
|---|---|---|---|---|---|---|---|---|---|---|---|
| 1 | | Stage By Stage (USA) | 14 | M L W Bell | 2 | 9-0 | Micky Fenton | 9/4 | | — | 88 |
| 2 | 4 | Esteemed Master (USA) | 2 | G A Butler | 2 | 9-0 | K Fallon | 15/8F | 80 | — | 81 |
| 3 | 2½ | Keetchy (IRE) | 3 | J L Dunlop | 2 | 9-0 | Pat Eddery | 2/1 | | — | 77 |
| 4 | 1¾ | Orthodox | 12 | G L Moore | 2 | 9-0 | Richard Hughes | 25/1 | | — | 73 |
| 5 | ¾ | Shove Ha'Penny (IRE) | 11 | N A Callaghan | 2 | 9-0 | Jimmy Fortune | 14/1 | 73 | — | 72 |
| 6 | ¾ | Extremist (USA) | 10 | R Hannon | 2 | 9-0 | Dane O'Neill | 20/1 | | — | 71 |
| 7 | 1 | Sergeant Cecil | 7 | J W Mullins | 2 | 9-0 | S Righton | 100/1 | | — | 69 |
| 8 | 1 | Silver Prophet (IRE) | 9 | K McAuliffe | 2 | 9-0 | G Hind | 33/1 | 72 | — | 67 |

| | | | Draw | TRAINER | Age | Wgt | JOCKEY | SP | OR | TS | RPR |
|---|---|---|---|---|---|---|---|---|---|---|---|
| 9 | 4 | **Murzim** | 8 | G A Butler | 2 | 9-0 | Vince Slattery | 50/1 | — | | 60 |
| 10 | 1½ | **Jumeirah Song (USA)** | 13 | M R Channon | 2 | 9-0 | Steve Drowne | 50/1 | — | | 57 |
| 11 | ½ | **Kingston Blue** | 6 | W G M Turner | 2 | 8-7 | L P Keniry(7) | 100/1 | — | | 56 |
| 12 | 15 | **L For Leisure** | 1 | W G M Turner | 2 | 9-0 | Alan Daly | 100/1 | — | | 29 |
| 13 | 18 | **Taranog** | 5 | B Palling | 2 | 8-11 | George Baker(3) | 66/1 | — | | — |
| 14 | 1¾ | **Royal Eberspacher (IRE)** | 4 | Mrs P N Dutfield | 2 | 8-9 | Allan Mackay | 100/1 | — | | — |

**14 ran** TIME 2m 12.40s (slow by 4.40s)   **TOTAL SP** 126%

# LINGFIELD (A.W)
27 March 2002
Standard

## 2:00 Greyhound Racing Association Maiden Stakes (Class D) (Div I) (Class 4) (3yo+) 1m2f
[off 2:03]   £2,964.00, £912.00, £456.00, £228.00

| | | | Draw | TRAINER | Age | Wgt | JOCKEY | SP | OR | TS | RPR |
|---|---|---|---|---|---|---|---|---|---|---|---|
| 1 | | **Charlie Simmons (IRE)** | 3 | A P Jarvis | 4 | 9-11 | K Fallon | 10/1 | 75 | 73 | 78 |
| 2 | hd | **Frankies Dream (IRE)** | 10 | T G Mills | 3 | 8-5 | Jimmy Quinn | 13/8F | | 69 | 78 |
| 3 | 2 | **Another Glimpse (GB)** | 6 | Miss B Sanders | 4 | 9-11 | N Callan | 50/1 | 63 | 69 | 74 |
| 4 | ½ | **Classic Example** | 5 | E A L Dunlop | 3 | 8-5 | W Ryan | 14/1 | | 64 | 73 |
| 5 | hd | **System** | 9 | B W Hills | 3 | 8-5 | Michael Hills | 5/2 | | 64 | 73 |
| 6 | 2½ | **Liszt (USA)** | 1 | G L Moore | 5 | 9-11 | Jimmy Fortune | 40/1 | | 63 | 68 |
| 7 | nk | **Alafzar (IRE)** | 7 | P D Evans | 4 | 9-11 t | Dane O'Neill | 25/1 | 66 | 63 | 67 |
| 8 | nk | **Fraternize** | 2 | S Dow | 4 | 9-11 | Chris Catlin | 16/1 | 65 | 63 | 67 |
| 9 | nk | **Sergeant Cecil** | 12 | J W Mullins | 3 | 8-5 | S Righton | 25/1 | | 59 | 66 |
| 10 | hd | **Passing Interest (USA)** | 8 | Mrs A J Perrett | 3 | 8-5 | Joe Fanning | 7/2 | | 59 | 66 |
| 11 | 14 | **Make My Hay (GB)** | 4 | J Cullinan | 3 | 8-5 | Neil Pollard | 66/1 | | 31 | 39 |
| 12 | 9 | **Valdasho** | 11 | G G Margarson | 3 | 8-0 | G Bardwell | 100/1 | | — | 17 |
| 13 | 22 | **Wild Times** | 14 | J C Fox | 6 | 9-8 | Pat Dobbs(3) | 100/1 | 20 | — | — |
| 14 | dist | **Thundering Jay-Sea** | 13 | J R Jenkins | 4 | 9-6 | Seb Sanders | 14/1 | | — | — |

**14 ran** TIME 2m 5.35s (slow by 0.15s)   **TOTAL SP** 132%

# SALISBURY
5 May 2002
Good To Firm

## 5:10 City Cabs Salisbury Maiden Stakes (Class D) (Class 4) (3yo) 1m4f
[off 5:16]   £4,290.00, £1,320.00, £660.00, £330.00

| | | | Draw | TRAINER | Age | Wgt | JOCKEY | SP | OR | TS | RPR |
|---|---|---|---|---|---|---|---|---|---|---|---|
| 1 | | **Gulf (IRE)** | 14 | D R C Elsworth | 3 | 9-0 | Dane O'Neill | 25/1 | | 61 | 82 |
| 2 | 1¼ | **Serotonin** | 4 | R Charlton | 3 | 9-0 | Eddie Ahern | 11/10F | | 58 | 81 |
| 3 | shd | **Ticket To Dance (IRE)** | 9 | J H M Gosden | 3 | 8-9 | Robert Havlin | 9/1 | | 53 | 75 |
| 4 | 3 | **Navale (FR)** | 8 | J H M Gosden | 3 | 8-9 | Seb Sanders | 20/1 | | 47 | 71 |
| 5 | 5 | **Red Halo** | 13 | R Hannon | 3 | 8-11 | Pat Dobbs(3) | 12/1 | 75 | 42 | 68 |
| 6 | ½ | **Queen Excalibur** | 15 | H R A Cecil | 3 | 8-9 | W Ryan | 9/1 | | 36 | 63 |
| 7 | nk | **Mount Street (IRE)** | 3 | Sir Michael Stoute | 3 | 8-9 | Paul Eddery | 9/4 | | 35 | 62 |
| 8 | 1¼ | **Cool Bathwick (IRE)** | 2 | E J O'Neill | 3 | 9-0 | John Egan | 33/1 | | 37 | 65 |
| 9 | shd | **Elle Royal (IRE)** | 6 | T P McGovern | 3 | 8-9 | Martin Dwyer | 50/1 | 72 | 32 | 60 |
| 10 | ¾ | **Sergeant Cecil** | 16 | J W Mullins | 3 | 9-0 | S Righton | 66/1 | 70 | 35 | 64 |
| 11 | 1 | **Pauluke** | 1 | N J Hawke | 3 | 8-9 | Alan Daly | 66/1 | | 28 | 58 |
| 12 | 12 | **Secret Flutter (IRE)** | 5 | J G Portman | 3 | 8-9 | Francis Norton | 50/1 | | — | 40 |
| 13 | 1¾ | **Harlestone Bay (GB)** | 12 | J L Dunlop | 3 | 9-0 | Paul Doe | 33/1 | | — | 42 |
| 14 | 2 | **Kamakazi Knight (IRE)** | 11 | R M Flower | 3 | 8-11 | Stephen Carson(3) | 100/1 | 35 | — | 39 |
| 15 | 1¼ | **Jevington Grey** | 17 | R M Flower | 3 | 9-0 | C Rutter | 100/1 | | — | 37 |

| | | | Draw | TRAINER | | | | JOCKEY | SP | OR | TS | RPR |
|---|---|---|---|---|---|---|---|---|---|---|---|---|
| 16 | ½ | **Kew** | 10 | J J Bridger | | 3 | 8-7 | Amir Quinn(7) | 100/1 | 42 | — | 36 |
| **17** | **dist** | **Business** | 7 | I A Wood | | 3 | 9-0 | N Callan | 66/1 | — | — | — |

**17 ran** TIME 2m 35.88s (slow by 2.88s)  **TOTAL SP** 131%

# SALISBURY

16 May 2002

Good

### 5:45 West Berkshire Racing Club Handicap (Class D) (Class 4) (3yo+,0–80) 1m4f

[off 5:45]  £4,504.50, £1,386.00, £693.00, £346.50

| | | | Draw | TRAINER | Age | Wgt | JOCKEY | SP | OR | TS | RPR |
|---|---|---|---|---|---|---|---|---|---|---|---|
| 1 | | **Showpiece** | 10 | W J Haggas | 4 | 9-0 | J Murtagh | 10/1 | 65 | 67 | 82+ |
| 2 | ½ | **Dr Cool** | 2 | J Akehurst | 5 | 8-13 | Jimmy Quinn | 9/4F | 64 | 65 | 74 |
| 3 | 1½ | **Fraternize** | 20 | S Dow | 4 | 9-2 | Chris Catlin | 11/1 | 67 | 65 | 75 |
| 4 | 2 | **Amir Zaman** | 18 | J W Payne | 4 | 8-13 | Michael Tebbutt | 12/1 | 64 | 58 | 69+ |
| 5 | 1¼ | **Aveiro (IRE)** | 4 | C P Morlock | 6 | 8-2 b | Francis Norton | 8/1 | 53 | 44 | 56 |
| 6 | 4 | **Fletcher** | 7 | H Morrison | 8 | 8-3 | L P Keniry(7) | 10/1 | 61 | 44 | 58 |
| 7 | hd | **Indian Beat** | 3 | C L Popham | 5 | 8-0 1 | Alan Daly | 25/1 | 51 | 33 | 48 |
| 8 | 2½ | **Follow Your Star** | 16 | P W Harris | 4 | 9-2 | Eddie Ahern | 20/1 | 67 | 45 | 60 |
| 9 | ½ | **Sergeant Cecil** | 13 | J W Mullins | 3 | 8-2 | Martin Dwyer | 33/1 | 70 | 46 | 62 |
| 10 | 2 | **Pinot Noir** | 6 | H Morrison | 4 | 9-10 | Steve Drowne | 12/1 | 75 | 48 | 64 |
| 11 | shd | **Absolute Utopia (USA)** | 17 | E A Wheeler | 9 | 7-13 | Matthew Henry | 16/1 | 50 | 23 | 39 |
| 12 | 2 | **Bold Ewar (IRE)** | 15 | C E Brittain | 5 | 9-0 | Royston Ffrench | 20/1 | 65 | 34 | 51 |
| 13 | 2 | **St Matthew (USA)** | 5 | J W Hills | 4 | 9-3 | Michael Hills | 14/1 | 68 | 33 | 51 |
| 14 | ¾ | **Darcy** | 12 | D C O'Brien | 8 | 9-10 | Seb Sanders | 100/1 | 75 | 38 | 57 |
| 15 | ¾ | **Porak (IRE)** | 1 | G L Moore | 5 | 9-2 | Ian Mongan | 20/1 | 67 | 28 | 48 |
| 16 | 1 | **Capriolo (IRE)** | 14 | J C Fox | 6 | 8-11 b | Pat Dobbs(3) | 12/1 | 65 | 24 | 44 |
| 17 | shd | **Arc En Ciel** | 8 | Mrs L Richards | 4 | 9-7 | Micky Fenton | 20/1 | 72 | 31 | 51 |
| 18 | 5 | **Forest Light (IRE)** | 9 | R F Johnson Houghton | 4 | 8-6 b | Richard Mullen | 14/1 | 57 | 6 | 29 |
| 19 | 5 | **Adjawar (IRE)** | 11 | C A Dwyer | 4 | 9-13 | Dane O'Neill | 20/1 | 78 | 17 | 42 |

**19 ran** TIME 2m 34.83s (slow by 1.83s)  **TOTAL SP** 142%

# SANDOWN

15 June 2002

Good

### 4:20 Melbourne Racing Club Handicap (Class D) (Class 4) (3yo+,0–80) 1m6f

[off 4:21]  £4,270.50, £1,314.00, £657.00, £328.50

| | | | Draw | TRAINER | Age | Wgt | JOCKEY | SP | OR | TS | RPR |
|---|---|---|---|---|---|---|---|---|---|---|---|
| 1 | | **Classic Millennium** | 5 | W J Musson | 4 | 7-4 | Lisa Jones(7) | 7/1 | 47 | — | 56 |
| 2 | 1 | **Dr Cool** | 8 | J Akehurst | 5 | 8-12 | M Howard(7) | 5/2J | 69 | — | 77 |
| 3 | ½ | **Smarter Charter** | 3 | Mrs L Stubbs | 9 | 7-4 13 | Kristin Stubbs(7) | 10/1 | 47 | — | 54 |
| 4 | ½ | **Its Your Bid** | 7 | S Woodman | 4 | 8-0 42 | Martin Dwyer | 10/1 | 50 | — | 57 |
| 5 | ½ | **Amir Zaman** | 4 | J W Payne | 4 | 9-0 | K Fallon | 5/2J | 64 | — | 70 |
| 6 | 1½ | **Sergeant Cecil** | 1 | J W Mullins | 3 | 7-5 | Francis Ferris(5) | 33/1 | 65 | — | 69 |
| 7 | 5 | **Hernandita** | 6 | M C Pipe | 4 | 9-8 | Jimmy Fortune | 8/1 | 72 | — | 70 |
| 8 | 2½ | **Renzo (IRE)** | 2 | John A Harris | 9 | 9-13 | Philip Robinson | 7/1 | 77 | — | 71 |

**8 ran** TIME 3m 11.69s (slow by 12.69s)  **TOTAL SP** 114%

# CHEPSTOW

26 August 2002

Good

## 5:10 chepstow-racecourse.co.uk Handicap (Class E) (Class 5) (3yo+,0-70) (1m2f36y) 1m2f

[off 5:10]  £3,757.00, £1,156.00, £578.00, £289.00

| | | | Draw | TRAINER | Age | Wgt | JOCKEY | SP | OR | TS | RPR |
|---|---|---|---|---|---|---|---|---|---|---|---|
| 1 | | Lara Falana | 1 | J A Osborne | 4 | 9-7 | Martin Dwyer | 9/2 | 54 | 56 | 65+ |
| 2 | 3 | Sergeant Cecil | 10 | B R Millman | 3 | 9-8 | Pat Eddery | 10/1 | 63 | 59 | 69 |
| 3 | nk | Mythical King (IRE) | 7 | B Palling | 5 | 9-10 | Fergus Sweeney | 25/1 | 57 | 53 | 62 |
| 4 | 1½ | Petite Futee | 13 | D Haydn Jones | 3 | 9-6 | Robert Havlin | 4/1J | 61 | 54 | 64 |
| 5 | nk | Dom Shadeed | 2 | R J Baker | 7 | 8-5 | Francis Ferris(5) | 20/1 | 43 | 36 | 45 |
| 6 | 1¼ | Replacement Pet (IRE) | 6 | H S Howe | 5 | 8-7 b | G Sparkes(5) | 11/1 | 45 | 35 | 45 |
| 7 | 4 | Eight (IRE) | 16 | C G Cox | 6 | 9-3 | Steve Drowne | 9/1 | 50 | 32 | 43 |
| 8 | ¾ | Ben Kenobi | 8 | Mrs P Ford | 4 | 8-7 | Allan Mackay | 25/1 | 40 | 20 | 31 |
| 9 | 1 | Birth Of The Blues | 12 | A Charlton | 6 | 8-0 | L P Keniry(5) | 4/1J | 38 | 16 | 28 |
| 10 | ½ | Reminiscent (IRE) | 9 | R F Johnson Houghton | 3 | 9-9 b1 | Dane O'Neill | 20/1 | 64 | 41 | 53 |
| 11 | 6 | Mr Whizz | 3 | M R Bosley | 5 | 8-10 | Joanna Badger | 16/1 | 43 | 8 | 21 |
| 12 | 3 | Better Moment (IRE) | 11 | M C Pipe | 5 | 8-2 v | Hannah Cowper(7) | 12/1 | 42 | 1 | 15 |
| 13 | 13 | Fight The Feeling | 5 | J W Unett | 4 | 9-1 | Seb Sanders | 10/1 | 48 | — | — |
| 14 | 2 | Gainful | 14 | G F H Charles-Jones | 3 | 8-13 | T G McLaughlin | 50/1 | 54 | — | — |
| 15 | 2½ | Castlebridge | 15 | M D I Usher | 5 | 8-8 b | David McCabe | 16/1 | 41 | — | — |
| 16 | ½ | Sharp Soprano | 4 | B R Millman | 3 | 8-7 | Michael Tebbutt | 25/1 | 48 | — | — |

**16 ran** TIME 2m 8.20s (slow by 1.20s)  **TOTAL SP** 137%

Sergeant Cecil kept on strongly under the whip for a fair second, but this trip looked on the sharp side for a horse who raced over 14 furlongs last time and another 2f would seem to be a minimum requirement for him to be seen to best effect.

# BEVERLEY

18 September 2002

Good To Firm

## 4:20 Tote Bookmakers Handicap (Class E) (Class 5) (3yo,0-70) (1m4f16y) 1m4f

[off 4:20]  £5,239.00, £1,612.00, £806.00, £403.00

| | | | Draw | TRAINER | Age | Wgt | JOCKEY | SP | OR | TS | RPR |
|---|---|---|---|---|---|---|---|---|---|---|---|
| 1 | | Michaels Dream (IRE) | 10 | J Hetherton | 3 | 8-1 v | T Williams | 14/1 | 50 | 39 | 59 |
| 2 | nk | Dalblair (IRE) | 8 | J A Glover | 3 | 9-7 | Robert Winston | 15/2 | 70 | 59 | 79 |
| 3 | 1½ | Sergeant Cecil | 2 | B R Millman | 3 | 9-1 | W Woods | 7/1 | 64 | 50 | 71 |
| 4 | 1 | Forest Ridge | 14 | Mrs A J Perrett | 3 | 8-2 1 | Stephen Carson | 12/1 | 51 | 35 | 56 |
| 5 | 5 | Galanthus (USA) | 13 | L M Cumani | 3 | 8-5 b1 | Shane Kelly | 5/1 | 54 | 28 | 52 |
| 6 | ½ | Full House (IRE) | 7 | P F I Cole | 3 | 9-4 | Seb Sanders | 8/1 | 67 | 40 | 64 |
| 7 | 1 | Almnadia (IRE) | 11 | S Gollings | 3 | 8-7 | Tony Culhane | 16/1 | 56 | 27 | 52 |
| 8 | shd | Life Is Beautiful (IRE) | 12 | W H Tinning | 3 | 8-11 | John McAuley | 20/1 | 60 | 31 | 55 |
| 9 | 5 | Greatdream (IRE) | 9 | E J O'Neill | 3 | 8-3 | Joe Fanning | 16/1 | 52 | 13 | 40 |
| 10 | 1¼ | He's The One | 1 | P W Harris | 3 | 8-10 | Paul Hanagan | 14/1 | 59 | 17 | 45 |
| 11 | shd | Washington Pink (IRE) | 6 | C Grant | 3 | 8-8 | Adrian T Nicholls | 15/2 | 57 | 15 | 43 |
| 12 | ¾ | Darjingle | 4 | T D Easterby | 3 | 8-8 | Ted Durcan | 50/1 | 57 | 13 | 42 |
| 13 | nk | Beauchamp Quiz | 3 | G A Butler | 3 | 9-2 | Eddie Ahern | 100/30F | 65 | 21 | 49 |
| 14 | dist | Digdaga (USA) | 5 | Mrs S Lamyman | 3 | 8-3 | K Dalgleish | 50/1 | 52 | — | — |

**14 ran** TIME 2m 40.50s (slow by 7.00s)  **TOTAL SP** 128%

Sergeant Cecil stayed on well without matching the winner's finishing burst and could be worth another try at a mile and three-quarters.

# SALISBURY

2 October 2002

Good To Soft

## 4:20 Denise & Peter Macklin Handicap (Class E) (Class 5) (3yo+,0-70) (1m6f15y) 1m6f

[off 4:20] £3,981.25, £1,225.00, £612.50, £306.25

| | | | Draw | TRAINER | Age | Wgt | JOCKEY | SP | OR | TS | RPR |
|---|---|---|---|---|---|---|---|---|---|---|---|
| 1 | | **Bobsleigh** | 17 | Mrs A J Perrett | 3 | 9-10 | Steve Drowne | 9/2F | 69 | 51 | 80 |
| 2 | nk | **Sergeant Cecil** | 11 | B R Millman | 3 | 9-6 | W Woods | 6/1 | 65 | 47 | 75 |
| 3 | shd | **Heir To Be** | 16 | J L Dunlop | 3 | 9-3 | W Ryan | 12/1 | 62 | 44 | 72 |
| 4 | 2 | **Nandoo** | 15 | P W Harris | 3 | 7-7 | Francis Ferris(5) | 20/1 | 43 | 21 | 51 |
| 5 | ½ | **Route Barree (FR)** | 13 | S Dow | 4 | 9-7 | Paul Doe | 11/1 | 57 | 34 | 64 |
| 6 | 6 | **Gold Standard (IRE)** | 9 | D R C Elsworth | 4 | 9-10 | Stephen Carson | 16/1 | 60 | 25 | 59 |
| 7 | ½ | **Branston Nell** | 4 | I A Wood | 3 | 9-3 | Jimmy Fortune | 9/1 | 62 | 26 | 61 |
| 8 | 5 | **Pauluke** | 14 | N J Hawke | 3 | 8-13 | Alan Daly | 25/1 | 58 | 12 | 50 |
| 9 | 3 | **Giko** | 10 | Jane Southcombe | 8 | 8-4 1 | Simon Whitworth | 33/1 | 40 | — | 28 |
| 10 | 2 | **Anniversary Guest (IRE)** | 2 | Lucinda Featherstone | 3 | 7-13 11 | C Rutter | 25/1 | 44 | — | 30 |
| 11 | 1 | **Irie Rasta (IRE)** | 7 | S Kirk | 3 | 9-8 | Dane O'Neill | 5/1 | 67 | — | 51 |
| 12 | shd | **Bid Me Welcome** | 1 | Miss D A McHale | 6 | 8-4 | Martin Dwyer | 12/1 | 40 | — | 24 |
| 13 | ½ | **Ella Carisa** | 12 | A Charlton | 3 | 7-13 11 | Royston Ffrench | 20/1 | 44 | — | 27 |
| 14 | 4 | **Physical Force** | 5 | J R Best | 4 | 9-1 | R Lake(7) | 14/1 | 58 | — | 36 |

**14 ran** TIME 3m 6.04s (slow by 5.04s) **TOTAL SP** 115%

Sergeant Cecil was stepping up in trip for the first time for his new trainer and again ran well. He should be rewarded for his consistency in another ordinary event.

# BATH

16 October 2002

Good

## 4:15 bath-racecourse.co.uk Handicap (Class D) (Class 4) (3yo+,0-80) (1m3f144y) 1m3½f

[off 4:16] £4,836.00, £1,488.00, £744.00, £372.00

| | | | Draw | TRAINER | Age | Wgt | JOCKEY | SP | OR | TS | RPR |
|---|---|---|---|---|---|---|---|---|---|---|---|
| 1 | | **Red Wine** | 7 | J A Osborne | 3 | 9-8 | Graham Gibbons | 10/1 | 76 | 80 | 88 |
| 2 | hd | **Sergeant Cecil** | 19 | B R Millman | 3 | 9-0 | Richard Hughes | 11/2F | 68 | 72 | 79 |
| 3 | 3½ | **Alfano (IRE)** | 16 | P Mitchell | 4 | 8-10 | John Egan | 20/1 | 57 | 54 | 63 |
| 4 | 7 | **Mystic Forest** | 3 | B J Meehan | 3 | 9-3 | Chris Catlin | 8/1 | 71 | 54 | 67 |
| 5 | ½ | **Shotacross The Bow (IRE)** | 17 | M Blanshard | 5 | 8-3 | David Kinsella(3) | 12/1 | 53 | 35 | 48 |
| 6 | 1 | **Desert City** | 9 | R Hannon | 3 | 9-1 | Dane O'Neill | 20/1 | 69 | 49 | 62 |
| 7 | 1¼ | **Knocktopher Abbey** | 14 | B R Millman | 5 | 9-4 b | Paul Hanagan | 16/1 | 65 | 42 | 56 |
| 8 | hd | **Shasta** | 18 | R M Beckett | 3 | 9-2 | Fergus Sweeney | 10/1 | 70 | 47 | 61 |
| 9 | 4 | **Toberoe Commotion (IRE)** | 12 | W R Muir | 4 | 8-9 | Richard Mullen | 33/1 | 56 | 25 | 41 |
| 10 | shd | **Adirika (IRE)** | 5 | Sir Michael Stoute | 3 | 9-7 v1 | Fergal Lynch | 7/1 | 75 | 44 | 60 |
| 11 | 3½ | **Spring Pursuit** | 15 | R J Price | 6 | 8-6 | Brett Doyle | 7/1 | 53 | 15 | 33 |
| 12 | nk | **Storm Seeker** | 1 | B W Hills | 3 | 9-10 | W Supple | 20/1 | 78 | 40 | 57 |
| 13 | nk | **Real Estate** | 10 | J S King | 8 | 8-3 | Hayley Turner(7) | 50/1 | 57 | 19 | 36 |
| 14 | nk | **Firestone (GER)** | 11 | A W Carroll | 5 | 8-13 | Dean Corby(5) | 25/1 | 65 | 27 | 43 |
| 15 | ½ | **Stratosphere** | 4 | I A Balding | 3 | 9-7 | Pat Eddery | 6/1 | 75 | 36 | 53 |
| 16 | ½ | **Anikitos (GB)** | 13 | Mrs A J Perrett | 4 | 10-0 | Stephen Carson | 25/1 | 75 | 35 | 52 |
| 17 | 11 | **Ski For Me (IRE)** | 2 | J L Dunlop | 3 | 9-12 | Paul Doe | 16/1 | 80 | 18 | 40 |
| 18 | 1¾ | **Pauluke** | 6 | N J Hawke | 3 | 8-1 b1 | Matthew Henry | 50/1 | 55 | — | 13 |

**18 ran** TIME 2m 30.00s (slow by 1.50s) **TOTAL SP** 132%

Sergeant Cecil once again got picked up after appearing to have the race won. He keeps creeping up the handicap as a result of placed efforts but deserves to win one of these for his consistency.

# WINDSOR

28 October 2002

Good To Soft

**4:15 Osram Handicap (Class D) (Class 4) (3yo,0–80)** (1m3f135y) 1m3½f

[off 4:15] £5,031.00, £1,548.00, £774.00, £387.00

| | | | Draw | TRAINER | Age | Wgt | JOCKEY | SP | OR | TS | RPR |
|---|---|---|---|---|---|---|---|---|---|---|---|
| 1 | | Mystic Mile (IRE) | 10 | M A Jarvis | 3 | 9-7 | N Callan | 9/1 | 80 | 53 | 9 |
| 2 | 1½ | Sergeant Cecil (GB) | 13 | B R Millman | 3 | 8-12 | W Woods | 4/1F | 71 | 41 | 79 |
| 3 | 1 | Olimolimoo (IRE) | 6 | M J Haynes | 3 | 8-12 | L P Keniry(5) | 14/1 | 76 | 44 | 82 |
| 4 | hd | Our Imperial Bay (USA) | 11 | Mrs A J Perrett | 3 | 8-11 b | Steve Drowne | 9/2 | 70 | 38 | 76 |
| 5 | nk | Factor Fifteen | 7 | E A L Dunlop | 3 | 9-0 | Joe Fanning | 7/1 | 73 | 41 | 78 |
| 6 | ¾ | Sabreline | 3 | D W P Arbuthnot | 3 | 7-5 3 | Frankie McDonald(7) | 25/1 | 57 | 23 | 61 |
| 7 | 1¾ | Kelpie (IRE) | 12 | I A Balding | 3 | 8-6 | Martin Dwyer | 14/1 | 65 | 27 | 67 |
| 8 | ½ | Miss Gigi | 17 | M R Channon | 3 | 8-11 | Chris Catlin | 12/1 | 70 | 31 | 71 |
| 9 | 1¼ | Zarza Bay (IRE) | 14 | K R Burke | 3 | 7-12 v1 | David Kinsella(3) | 10/1 | 60 | 18 | 59 |
| 10 | shd | Bualadhbos (IRE) | 1 | F Jordan | 3 | 7-12 | Robyn Brisland | 33/1 | 57 | 15 | 52 |
| 11 | hd | Full House (IRE) | 15 | P F I Cole | 3 | 8-6 | Oscar Urbina | 8/1 | 65 | 23 | 61 |
| 12 | 1 | Murzim | 4 | J Gallagher | 3 | 9-5 | Eddie Ahern | 12/1 | 78 | 34 | 75 |
| 13 | 1 | Ski For Me (IRE) | 16 | J L Dunlop | 3 | 9-3 | Paul Doe | 14/1 | 76 | 30 | 72 |
| 14 | 2 | Secret Flutter (IRE) | 9 | J G Portman | 3 | 7-12 | Paul Quinn | 40/1 | 57 | — | 49 |
| 15 | 6 | Zigali (GB) | 8 | P S McEntee | 3 | 7-12 12 | Stephen Davies | 50/1 | 57 | — | 40 |
| 16 | 4 | Mrs Pooters (IRE) | 2 | D W P Arbuthnot | 3 | 8-1 5 | Ryan Moore(5) | 33/1 | 65 | — | 4 |
| 17 | dist | The Copt | 5 | J M P Eustace | 3 | 8-2 | J Tate | 33/1 | 61 | — | — |

**17 ran** TIME 2m 35.05s (slow by 8.15s) **TOTAL SP** 133%

Sergeant Cecil came through to have every chance in the final two furlongs but could only stay on at the same pace. He looks capable of winning a race but has been creeping up the ratings without getting off the mark.

# WINDSOR

7 April 2003

Good To Firm

**3:45 Quality Heating Services Handicap (Class D) (Class 4) (3yo+,0–85)** (1m3f135y) 1m3½f

[off 3:47] £5,736.25, £1,765.00, £882.50, £441.25

| | | | Draw | TRAINER | Age | Wgt | JOCKEY | SP | OR | TS | RPR |
|---|---|---|---|---|---|---|---|---|---|---|---|
| 1 | | Palamedes | 11 | P W Harris | 4 | 9-5 | Eddie Ahern | 20/1 | 76 | 79 | 86 |
| 2 | shd | Sergeant Cecil | 6 | B R Millman | 4 | 9-2 | Darryll Holland | 9/2J | 73 | 76 | 83 |
| 3 | 2 | Silvaline | 3 | T Keddy | 4 | 8-10 | G Carter | 25/1 | 67 | 66 | 74 |
| 4 | 1½ | Frontier | 8 | B J Llewellyn | 6 | 8-12 | Steve Drowne | 33/1 | 68 | 64 | 73 |
| 5 | 2 | Fast Foil (IRE) | 10 | M R Channon | 5 | 9-0 | Edward Creighton(5) | 6/1 | 75 | 67 | 77 |
| 6 | nk | Amigo (IRE) | 9 | P Mitchell | 5 | 9-5 | K Fallon | 9/2J | 75 | 67 | 76 |
| 7 | 1 | Classic Role | 1 | R Ingram | 4 | 9-3 | Fergus Sweeney | 12/1 | 74 | 64 | 74 |
| 8 | 2½ | Castleshane (IRE) | 12 | S Gollings | 6 | 9-8 | J-P Guillambert(5) | 9/1 | 83 | 68 | 79 |
| 9 | nk | True Thunder | 15 | Julian Poulton | 6 | 9-5 | R J Molloy(7) | 33/1 | 82 | 67 | 78 |
| 10 | 1¼ | Attorney General (IRE) | 14 | J A B Old | 4 | 9-11 | Seb Sanders | 16/1 | 82 | 64 | 76 |
| 11 | nk | Stunning Force (IRE) | 13 | M Johnston | 4 | 9-12 | K Darley | 11/2 | 83 | 65 | 76 |
| 12 | 7 | Royal Prodigy (USA) | 2 | M C Pipe | 4 | 8-9 | J D Smith | 11/2 | 66 | 34 | 49 |
| 13 | dist | Adronikus (IRE) | 7 | D J Wintle | 6 | 9-13 tb | Ian Mongan | 33/1 | 83 | — | — |
| 14 | 2 | Tasneef (USA) | 4 | T D McCarthy | 4 | 9-5 | Chris Catlin | 20/1 | 76 | — | — |

**14 ran** TIME 2m 29.71s (slow by 2.81s) **TOTAL SP** 127%

Sergeant Cecil is still a maiden and was finishing second for the fifth time in his last six starts. However, he did not appear to do anything wrong and his turn should come one day.

# NEWMARKET

16 April 2003

Good To Firm

## 5:10 Babraham Handicap (Class C) (Class 3) (4yo+,0-95) 1m4f

[off 5:12] £9,685.00, £2,980.00, £1,490.00, £745.00

| | | | Draw | TRAINER | Age | Wgt | JOCKEY | SP | OR | TS | RPR |
|---|---|---|---|---|---|---|---|---|---|---|---|
| 1 | | Chai Walla | 7 | H R A Cecil | 4 | 9-7 | T Quinn | 2/1F | 88 | 87 | 99 |
| 2 | 1¼ | Shami | 4 | D R Loder | 4 | 10-0 v | L Dettori | 6/1 | 95 | 91 | 104 |
| 3 | 1 | Flotta | 11 | M R Channon | 4 | 8-7 | Edward Creighton(5) | 4/1 | 79 | 73 | 86 |
| 4 | nk | Big Moment | 9 | Mrs A J Perrett | 5 | 9-12 | Pat Eddery | 14/1 | 92 | 86 | 99+ |
| 5 | ½ | Ampoule | 10 | C E Brittain | 4 | 8-3 | Jimmy Quinn | 33/1 | 70 | 63 | 76 |
| 6 | ½ | Fourth Dimension (IRE) | 1 | A C Stewart | 4 | 8-11 | K Fallon | 14/1 | 78 | 70 | 83+ |
| 7 | ¾ | Ring Of Destiny | 3 | P W Harris | 4 | 9-8 | W Supple | 20/1 | 89 | 79 | 93 |
| 8 | 1¾ | Beat The Heat (IRE) | 8 | Jedd O'Keeffe | 5 | 9-1 | Richard Hughes | 50/1 | 81 | 67 | 82 |
| 9 | 5 | Allinjim (IRE) | 5 | J A Glover | 4 | 9-2 p | Seb Sanders | 14/1 | 83 | 59 | 76 |
| 10 | 9 | Sergeant Cecil | 6 | B R Millman | 4 | 8-6 p | Darryll Holland | 4/1 | 73 | 31 | 52 |
| 11 | 28 | Bound | 2 | Mrs L Wadham | 5 | 8-6 | Jamie Spencer | 33/1 | 72 | — | 6 |

**11 ran** TIME 2m 34.40s (slow by 6.70s) **TOTAL SP** 120%

# SANDOWN

27 May 2003

Good To Firm

## 8:15 Betting Brain Has Evolved Handicap (Class D) (Class 4) (3yo+,0-85) 1m6f

[off 8:18] £5,655.00, £1,740.00, £870.00, £435.00

| | | | Draw | TRAINER | Age | Wgt | JOCKEY | SP | OR | TS | RPR |
|---|---|---|---|---|---|---|---|---|---|---|---|
| 1 | | Sergeant Cecil | 12 | B R Millman | 4 | 9-7 | Richard Hughes | 12/1 | 76 | — | 87 |
| 2 | 1¼ | Reveillez | 2 | J R Fanshawe | 4 | 9-11 | Oscar Urbina | 4/1 | 80 | — | 89 |
| 3 | nk | Manoubi | 7 | Sir Michael Stoute | 4 | 9-11 | K Fallon | 5/4F | 80 | — | 89 |
| 4 | 1¼ | Splash Out Again | 3 | H Morrison | 5 | 8-7 | Steve Drowne | 13/2 | 62 | — | 69+ |
| 5 | ½ | We'll Make It (IRE) | 10 | G L Moore | 5 | 8-2 b | Ryan Moore(3) | 25/1 | 60 | — | 66 |
| 6 | ½ | Sudden Flight (IRE) | 9 | R Ingram | 6 | 8-12 | Nigel Day | 16/1 | 67 | — | 73 |
| 7 | ¾ | Triplemoon (USA) | 11 | P W Harris | 4 | 8-6 | T Quinn | 10/1 | 61 | — | 66 |
| 8 | 1¼ | Afadan (IRE) | 5 | J R Jenkins | 5 | 9-11 | K Darley | 25/1 | 80 | — | 83 |
| 9 | ¾ | Danakil | 6 | S Dow | 8 | 9-10 | Paul Doe | 14/1 | 79 | — | 81 |
| 10 | ½ | Mumbling (IRE) | 1 | M H Tompkins | 5 | 9-9 | Ted Durcan | 14/1 | 78 | — | 79 |

**10 ran** TIME 3m 10.57s (slow by 11.57s) **TOTAL SP** 121%

SERGEANT CECIL had disappointed when tried in cheekpieces at Newmarket, and they were left off, although Rod Millman also pointed out that he had been knocked about there, which was also a factor. He had been very consistent, if frustrating, previously, and he was entitled to be thereabouts again.

# SANDOWN

14 June 2003

Good To Firm

## 4:30 Melbourne Racing Club Handicap (Class D) (Class 4) (3yo+,0-80) 1m6f

[off 4:34] £5,671.25, £1,745.00, £872.50, £436.25

| | | | Draw | TRAINER | Age | Wgt | JOCKEY | SP | OR | TS | RPR |
|---|---|---|---|---|---|---|---|---|---|---|---|
| 1 | | Sindapour (IRE) | 5 | M C Pipe | 5 | 9-1 | Martin Dwyer | 15/2 | 67 | 39 | 77 |
| 2 | 1 | Sergeant Cecil | 8 | B R Millman | 4 | 9-13 | Jimmy Fortune | 7/1 | 79 | 49 | 88 |
| 3 | shd | Fourth Dimension (IRE) | 10 | A C Stewart | 4 | 9-12 | Jamie Spencer | 6/4F | 78 | 48 | 87 |
| 4 | 1¼ | Ocean Avenue (IRE) | 3 | C A Horgan | 4 | 9-9 | W Woods | 15/2 | 75 | 42 | 82 |
| 5 | 3 | Tass Heel (IRE) | 9 | M R Channon | 4 | 8-2 | Chris Catlin | 9/1 | 54 | 15 | 57 |
| 6 | 1½ | Almaydan | 7 | R Lee | 5 | 9-10 | Pat Eddery | 11/1 | 76 | 34 | 77 |
| 7 | hd | Tasneef (USA) | 2 | T D McCarthy | 4 | 8-11 | Brett Doyle | 25/1 | 63 | 21 | 64 |
| 8 | nk | King Flyer (IRE) | 1 | Miss J Feilden | 7 | 9-12 t | Shane Kelly | 11/1 | 78 | 36 | 78 |

| | | | Draw | TRAINER | Age | Wgt | JOCKEY | SP | OR | TS | RPR |
|---|---|---|---|---|---|---|---|---|---|---|---|
| 9 | 1 | **Classic Millennium** | 12 | W J Musson | 5 | 7-7 2 | Lisa Jones(5) | 14/1 | 50 | — | 49 |
| 10 | ½ | **We'll Make It (IRE)** | 4 | G L Moore | 5 | 8-4 b | Ryan Moore(3) | 14/1 | 59 | 14 | 57 |
| 11 | 8 | **Kaluana Court** | 11 | R J Price | 7 | 7-12 3 | Dean Mernagh | 12/1 | 50 | — | 38 |
| 12 | dist | **Smarter Charter** | 6 | Mrs L Stubbs | 10 | 7-6 116 | Kristin Stubbs(7) | 66/1 | 50 | — | — |

**12 ran** TIME 2m 59.73s (slow by 0.73s)  **TOTAL SP** 129%

Sergeant Cecil ran another good race and might have repeated his recent course and distance win but for hanging right in the closing stages.

# SANDOWN

4 July 2003

Good

**4:50 Hampton Court Handicap (Class C) (Class 3) (3yo+,0–90)** 1m6f

[off 4:51] £9,977.50, £3,070.00, £1,535.00, £767.50

| | | | Draw | TRAINER | Age | Wgt | JOCKEY | SP | OR | TS | RPR |
|---|---|---|---|---|---|---|---|---|---|---|---|
| 1 | | **Sergeant Cecil** | 7 | B R Millman | 4 | 9-7 | Richard Hughes | 4/1J | 82 | — | 93 |
| 2 | ¾ | **Mr Ed (IRE)** | 1 | P Bowen | 5 | 9-0 | L Dettori | 9/2 | 75 | — | 85 |
| 3 | ¾ | **Albanov (IRE)** | 8 | J L Dunlop | 3 | 8-7 | K Fallon | 5/1 | 83 | — | 92 |
| 4 | ½ | **Sphinx (FR)** | 3 | Jamie Poulton | 5 | 9-2 | D O'Donohoe | 25/1 | 77 | — | 85 |
| 5 | nk | **Saint Alebe** | 4 | D R C Elsworth | 4 | 10-0 | T Quinn | 4/1J | 89 | — | 97+ |
| 6 | 1 | **Light Scent (USA)** | 10 | J Akehurst | 4 | 9-7 | Seb Sanders | 11/2 | 82 | — | 89 |
| 7 | 1½ | **Skylarker (USA)** | 2 | W S Kittow | 5 | 9-1 p | Darryll Holland | 11/1 | 76 | — | 81 |
| 8 | 5 | **Smyslov** | 6 | P R Webber | 5 | 8-9 v | Pat Dobbs | 33/1 | 70 | — | 68 |
| 9 | 3½ | **Haafel (USA)** | 9 | G L Moore | 6 | 8-4 b | Richard Mullen | 14/1 | 65 | — | 59 |
| 10 | 11 | **Caqui D'Or (IRE)** | 5 | J L Dunlop | 5 | 9-6 | Pat Eddery | 14/1 | 81 | — | 60 |

**10 ran** TIME 3m 7.19s (slow by 8.19s)  **TOTAL SP** 118%

A rather muddling race, Light Scent failing to set the anticipated strong pace and allowing Albanov to go past and slow it down down the far side. This played into the hands of SERGEANT CECIL, who is effective at shorter distances and was full of running 3f out. When switched to the inner for his challenge he soon took charge and went clear, and he held on well.

# ASCOT

12 July 2003

Good To Firm

**2:30 Tote Exacta Handicap (Class B) (Class 2) (3yo+,0–105)** (2m45y) 2m

[off 2:30] £37,700.00, £14,300.00, £7,150.00, £3,250.00, £1,625.00, £975.00

| | | | Draw | TRAINER | Age | Wgt | JOCKEY | SP | OR | TS | RPR |
|---|---|---|---|---|---|---|---|---|---|---|---|
| 1 | | **Mana D'Argent (IRE)** | 11 | M Johnston | 6 | 8-7 | Joe Fanning | 5/1F | 84 | — | 94 |
| 2 | ¾ | **Thewhirlingdervish (IRE)** | 12 | T D Easterby | 5 | 8-1 | Jimmy Quinn | 8/1 | 78 | — | 87 |
| 3 | 1½ | **Gulf (IRE)** | 10 | D R C Elsworth | 4 | 9-11 | L Dettori | 15/2 | 102 | 23 | 109 |
| 4 | nk | **Distinction (IRE)** | 5 | Sir Michael Stoute | 4 | 9-9 | C Soumillon | 13/2 | 100 | 21 | 107 |
| 5 | ¾ | **Moon Emperor** | 3 | J R Jenkins | 6 | 9-1 | W Ryan | 25/1 | 92 | 11 | 98 |
| 6 | shd | **Saint Alebe** | 7 | D R C Elsworth | 4 | 8-13 | Oscar Urbina | 11/1 | 90 | — | 96 |
| 7 | 2½ | **Zibeline (IRE)** | 14 | B R Millman | 6 | 8-10 p | Tony Hamilton(5) | 10/1 | 92 | — | 95 |
| 8 | 2½ | **Sergeant Cecil** | 4 | B R Millman | 4 | 8-10 | Richard Hughes | 10/1 | 87 | — | 87 |
| 9 | 2 | **Knavesmire Omen** | 13 | M Johnston | 4 | 9-2 | Simon Whitworth | 16/1 | 93 | — | 90 |
| 10 | 1¾ | **Red Wine** | 2 | J A Osborne | 4 | 9-4 | Martin Dwyer | 12/1 | 95 | — | 90 |
| 11 | 3½ | **Theatre (USA)** | 9 | Jamie Poulton | 4 | 8-8 | Steve Drowne | 12/1 | 85 | — | 76 |
| 12 | nk | **Indian Solitaire (IRE)** | 8 | R A Fahey | 4 | 7-12 | H Goto | 16/1 | 75 | — | 66 |
| 13 | ¾ | **Double Honour (FR)** | 1 | P J Hobbs | 5 | 9-8 | J-P Guillambert(5) | 16/1 | 104 | — | 94 |

**13 ran** TIME 3m 33.82s  **TOTAL SP** 116%

Sergeant Cecil surprisingly set the pace, albeit only a very moderate one and, although still going well turning in, was a spent force soon after.

# ASCOT

9 August 2003

Good To Firm

### 4:00 Carvill Shergar Cup Challenge (Class B) (Rated Stakes Handicap) (Class 2) (4yo+,0–100) 1m4f

[off 4:01] £20,000.00, £7,000.00, £3,200.00, £2,500.00, £2,200.00, £1,600.00

| | | | Draw | TRAINER | Age | Wgt | JOCKEY | SP | OR | TS | RPR |
|---|---|---|---|---|---|---|---|---|---|---|---|
| 1 | | Capitano Corelli (IRE) | 5 | P F I Cole | 4 | 8-11 t | S Dye | 20/1 | 88 | 76 | 96 |
| 2 | 3/4 | Sergeant Cecil | 9 | B R Millman | 4 | 8-10 | K Fallon | 8/1 | 87 | 73 | 94 |
| 3 | 1/2 | Muhareb (USA) | 4 | C E Brittain | 4 | 9-7 t | F Johansson | 10/1 | 98 | 83 | 104 |
| 4 | 3/4 | Reveillez (GB) | 6 | J R Fanshawe | 4 | 8-10 | Pat Eddery | 7/2F | 87 | 70 | 92 |
| 5 | 1/2 | Flownaway | 8 | W Jarvis | 4 | 9-6 | Darryll Holland | 12/1 | 97 | 79 | 101 |
| 6 | 1 3/4 | Courageous Duke (USA) | 7 | J Noseda | 4 | 9-6 | J Murtagh | 6/1 | 97 | 75 | 98 |
| 7 | 2 | Mamcazma (GB) | 10 | D Morris | 5 | 9-7 | L Dettori | 5/1 | 98 | 72 | 96 |
| 8 | 1 3/4 | Golden Lariat (USA) | 1 | Sir Michael Stoute | 4 | 8-10 | Y Take | 5/1 | 87 | 57 | 82 |
| 9 | 1 1/4 | Kylkenny | 2 | H Morrison | 8 | 8-7 1t | A Suborics | 9/1 | 84 | 51 | 77 |
| 10 | 11 | Vicious Prince (IRE) | 3 | R M Whitaker | 4 | 8-12 | M J Kinane | 33/1 | 89 | 34 | 65 |

**10 ran** TIME 2m 32.67s (slow by 2.67s)   **TOTAL SP** 115%

The winner and Muhareb effectively ended Sergeant Cecil's menacing move into the final furlong which saw him snatched up and switched to the far rail as the gap closed on him. His rider thought he was definitely robbed and, amazingly, the stewards only deemed Muhareb's jockey guilty of careless riding when both jockeys failed to switch whip hands with their horses tending to drift. Shane Dye was lucky to escape – cynics might say it saved the stewards having to make a judgement call on a winner possibly losing a race – as his mount was the one to edge most across the runner-up. Sergeant Cecil was readily held after, and is another who had looked plenty high enough in the handicap after a win last month, although this trip now looks on the sharp side.

# HAYDOCK

6 September 2003

Good To Firm

### 1:45 Freephone Stanley Old Borough Cup Stakes Showcase Handicap (Class C) (Class 3) (3yo+,0–90) 1m6f

[off 1:45] £32,500.00, £10,000.00, £5,000.00, £2,500.00

| | | | Draw | TRAINER | Age | Wgt | JOCKEY | SP | OR | TS | RPR |
|---|---|---|---|---|---|---|---|---|---|---|---|
| 1 | | The Persuader (IRE) | 10 | M Johnston | 3 | 8-2 | Joe Fanning | 11/2 | 75 | 45 | 86+ |
| 2 | nk | Star Member (IRE) | 12 | A P Jarvis | 4 | 9-0 | T Jarnet | 20/1 | 76 | 46 | 86 |
| 3 | 1 | Spectrometer | 13 | M Johnston | 6 | 9-8 | K Dalgleish | 10/1 | 84 | 52 | 93 |
| 4 | shd | Royal Cavalier | 7 | R Hollinshead | 6 | 9-11 | John Carroll | 14/1 | 87 | 55 | 96 |
| 5 | 1 1/4 | Random Quest | 11 | P F I Cole | 5 | 10-0 | K Darley | 9/1 | 90 | 55 | 97 |
| 6 | 5 | Ravenglass (USA) | 5 | J G M O'Shea | 4 | 9-8 | Adrian T Nicholls | 33/1 | 84 | 39 | 85 |
| 7 | nk | Constantine | 15 | J S Goldie | 3 | 8-3 1 | L P Keniry(3) | 14/1 | 79 | 33 | 79 |
| 8 | 3/4 | Prairie Falcon | 17 | B W Hills | 9 | 9-9 | Eddie Ahern | 25/1 | 85 | 38 | 85 |
| 9 | 2 1/2 | Duke Of Earl (IRE) | 9 | S Kirk | 4 | 9-5 | Dane O'Neill | 25/1 | 81 | 29 | 77 |
| 10 | 18 | Tiyoun (IRE) | 14 | Jedd O'Keeffe | 5 | 8-12 | Robert Winston | 14/1 | 74 | – | 47 |
| 11 | 2 1/2 | Ezz Elkheil | 1 | J W Payne | 4 | 9-2 | Simon Whitworth | 33/1 | 78 | – | 48 |
| 12 | 2 1/2 | Jack Dawson (IRE) | 16 | John Berry | 6 | 8-11 | Brett Doyle | 16/1 | 73 | – | 39 |
| 13 | nk | Thewhirlingdervish (IRE) | 8 | T D Easterby | 5 | 9-5 | W Supple | 20/1 | 81 | – | 47 |
| 14 | 1 1/4 | Mr Ed (IRE) | 4 | P Bowen | 5 | 9-0 b1 | Stephen Carson | 20/1 | 76 | – | 40 |
| 15 | 1 3/4 | Indian Solitaire (IRE) | 19 | R A Fahey | 4 | 8-11 | Paul Hanagan | 25/1 | 73 | – | 35 |
| 16 | 1/2 | Clarinch Claymore | 18 | J M Jefferson | 7 | 8-11 | Darren Williams | 33/1 | 73 | – | 34 |
| 17 | 9 | Sergeant Cecil | 20 | B R Millman | 4 | 9-13 | Richard Hughes | 10/1 | 89 | – | 39 |
| 18 | dist | Mac | 2 | M P Tregoning | 3 | 9-3 | Seb Sanders | 5/1F | 90 | – | – |
| 19 | dist | Stage By Stage (USA) | 6 | C R Egerton | 4 | 10-0 | Ted Durcan | 50/1 | 90 | – | – |

**19 ran** TIME 3m 4.25s (slow by 6.25s)   **TOTAL SP** 122%

Jockey Richard Hughes reported that Sergeant Cecil lost its action.

# EPSOM

21 April 2004

Soft

**2:55 bet@bluesq.com Great Metropolitan Stakes (Handicap) (Class C) (Class 3) (3yo+,0–95)** (1m4f10y) 1m4f

[off 2:58] £15,892.00, £6,028.00, £3,014.00, £1,370.00, £685.00, £411.00

| | | | Draw | TRAINER | Age | Wgt | JOCKEY | SP | OR | TS | RPR |
|---|---|---|---|---|---|---|---|---|---|---|---|
| 1 | | Cold Turkey | 14 | G L Moore | 4 | 8-12 | Simon Whitworth | 11/2F | 79 | 83 | 91 |
| 2 | 3 | General | 18 | N P Littmoden | 7 | 8-2 2 | T P Queally(3) | 20/1 | 71 | 69 | 79 |
| 3 | 1½ | Vengeance | 13 | Mrs A J Perrett | 4 | 9-9 | Dane O'Neill | 7/1 | 90 | 85 | 96 |
| 4 | ½ | Pagan Dance (IRE) | 11 | Mrs A J Perrett | 5 | 9-10 p | L Dettori | 9/1 | 90 | 85 | 95+ |
| 5 | 2 | Champion Lion (IRE) | 6 | M R Channon | 5 | 8-1 | Sam Hitchcott(3) | 14/1 | 70 | 61 | 72+ |
| 6 | ½ | Ofaraby | 2 | M A Jarvis | 4 | 9-5 | Philip Robinson | 13/2 | 86 | 76 | 88+ |
| 7 | 1½ | Lennel | 19 | A Bailey | 6 | 8-2 b | Francis Norton | 14/1 | 68 | 55 | 68 |
| 8 | 5 | Individual Talents (USA) | 8 | S C Williams | 4 | 8-2 | Martin Dwyer | 10/1 | 69 | 47 | 62 |
| 9 | 1 | Danakil | 3 | S Dow | 9 | 8-7 | Ryan Moore | 20/1 | 73 | 49 | 64 |
| 10 | 4 | Muskatsturm (GER) | 7 | B J Curley | 5 | 8-9 | Shane Kelly | 25/1 | 75 | 44 | 61 |
| 11 | 1 | Bucks | 16 | D K Ivory | 7 | 8-5 | Chris Catlin | 20/1 | 71 | 38 | 55 |
| 12 | 4 | Ezz Elkheil | 9 | J R Jenkins | 5 | 8-8 | Darryll Holland | 16/1 | 74 | 33 | 53 |
| 13 | 7 | Football Crazy (IRE) | 5 | P Bowen | 5 | 9-3 b | K Fallon | 14/1 | 83 | 29 | 52 |
| 14 | 10 | Persian King (IRE) | 15 | J A B Old | 7 | 9-1 | Steve Drowne | 50/1 | 81 | 7 | 36 |
| 15 | 10 | Mexican Pete | 12 | P W Hiatt | 4 | 8-6 | Robert Miles(3) | 33/1 | 76 | – | 17 |
| 16 | 3 | Jeepstar | 17 | T D Easterby | 4 | 8-10 | Jamie Mackay | 20/1 | 77 | – | 14 |
| 17 | 2 | Heisse | 10 | D R Loder | 4 | 10-0 v1 | J Murtagh | 12/1 | 95 | – | 29 |
| 18 | 8 | Stolen Hours (USA) | 4 | J Akehurst | 4 | 8-8 | T Quinn | 33/1 | 75 | – | – |
| 19 | 3½ | Lunar Leader (IRE) | 20 | M J Gingell | 4 | 7-9 p | Lisa Jones(3) | 50/1 | 65 | – | – |
| 20 | dist | Sergeant Cecil | 1 | B R Millman | 5 | 9-8 | Richard Hughes | 20/1 | 88 | – | – |

**20 ran** TIME 2m 53.93s (slow by 17.93s)　**TOTAL SP** 131%

# GOODWOOD

18 June 2004

Good To Firm

**7:50 Renault Van Stakes (Handicap) (Class D) (Class 4) (3yo+,0–85)** 1m4f

[off 7:51] £6,906.25, £2,125.00, £1,062.50, £531.25

| | | | Draw | TRAINER | Age | Wgt | JOCKEY | SP | OR | TS | RPR |
|---|---|---|---|---|---|---|---|---|---|---|---|
| 1 | | Wait For The Will (USA) | 8 | G L Moore | 8 | 9-6 b | Amir Quinn(5) | 8/1 | 82 | 81 | 92 |
| 2 | 1¾ | Northside Lodge (IRE) | 2 | P W Harris | 6 | 9-5 | W Supple | 6/1 | 76 | 72 | 83 |
| 3 | hd | Sergeant Cecil | 1 | B R Millman | 5 | 10-0 | Steve Drowne | 33/1 | 85 | 81 | 92 |
| 4 | ½ | Man At Arms (IRE) | 4 | R Hannon | 3 | 8-3 5 | Ryan Moore | 5/2 | 74 | 69 | 80 |
| 5 | 1½ | Winners Delight | 7 | A P Jarvis | 3 | 8-9 | Kerrin McEvoy | 16/1 | 80 | 72 | 84 |
| 6 | ½ | Sunny Glenn | 9 | Mrs P N Dutfield | 6 | 9-12 | Robert Havlin | 40/1 | 83 | 75 | 86 |
| 7 | 1¼ | Tidal | 3 | A W Carroll | 5 | 8-3 5 | Richard Thomas(5) | 7/4F | 65 | 54 | 66 |
| 8 | 5 | Desert Island Disc | 10 | J J Bridger | 7 | 8-13 | Frankie McDonald(3) | 16/1 | 73 | 54 | 66 |
| 9 | 10 | Private Benjamin | 5 | Jamie Poulton | 4 | 7-13 511 | Chris Catlin | 16/1 | 55 | 20 | 33 |
| 10 | 5 | Rainbow World (IRE) | 6 | Andrew Reid | 4 | 8-8 p | John Egan | 33/1 | 65 | 20 | 34 |
| 11 | 23 | Richemaur (IRE) | 11 | M H Tompkins | 4 | 9-2 | G Duffield | 14/1 | 73 | – | 5 |

**11 ran** TIME 2m 38.36s (slow by 3.76s)　**TOTAL SP** 122%

Sergeant Cecil weakened in the closing stages and was no match for the winner. He probably found the ground a bit lively and the trip looked inadequate.

# SANDOWN

2 July 2004

Good To Soft

### 4:50 Sundown At Sandown Handicap (Class C) (Class 3) (3yo+,0–90) 1m6f

[off 4:50] £9,750.00, £3,000.00, £1,500.00, £750.00

| | | | Draw | TRAINER | Age | Wgt | JOCKEY | SP | OR | TS | RPR |
|---|---|---|---|---|---|---|---|---|---|---|---|
| 1 | | Quedex | 7 | R J Price | 8 | 8-0 | Frankie McDonald(3) | 4/1 | 64 | 68 | 79 |
| 2 | 7 | Mr Ed (IRE) | 5 | P Bowen | 6 | 8-11 p | Dean Corby(3) | 7/2F | 75 | 69 | 84+ |
| 3 | shd | Theatre (USA) | 3 | Jamie Poulton | 5 | 9-8 | Paul Doe | 9/1 | 83 | 77 | 88 |
| 4 | 5 | Redspin (IRE) | 10 | J S Moore | 4 | 8-7 | Martin Dwyer | 14/1 | 68 | 54 | 66 |
| 5 | 5 | Sergeant Cecil | 6 | B R Millman | 5 | 9-11 | K Fallon | 4/1 | 86 | 65 | 77 |
| 6 | nk | Twofan (USA) | 9 | M Johnston | 3 | 8-6 | Stanley Chin | 5/1 | 82 | 61 | 73 |
| 7 | 10 | Flotta | 2 | M R Channon | 5 | 9-7 | Ted Durcan | 6/1 | 82 | 45 | 59 |

**7 ran** TIME 3m 10.31s (slow by 11.31s) **TOTAL SP** 109%

Last year's winner Sergeant Cecil spoilt his chance by pulling too hard, and he had nothing left for the finish.

# ASCOT

9 July 2004

Good

### 3:50 Sony Wega Handicap (Class C) (Class 3) (3yo+,0–90) 1m4f

[off 3:53] £9,782.50, £3,010.00, £1,505.00, £752.50

| | | | Draw | TRAINER | Age | Wgt | JOCKEY | SP | OR | TS | RPR |
|---|---|---|---|---|---|---|---|---|---|---|---|
| 1 | | Sergeant Cecil | 8 | B R Millman | 5 | 9-13 | Jimmy Fortune | 16/1 | 86 | 83 | 95 |
| 2 | shd | Cutting Crew (USA) | 10 | P W Harris | 3 | 9-4 | Darryll Holland | 4/1 | 90 | 87 | 99 |
| 3 | 1¼ | Fort | 2 | M Johnston | 3 | 9-1 | Stanley Chin | 11/1 | 87 | 82 | 94 |
| 4 | shd | Mexican Pete (GB) | 9 | P W Hiatt | 4 | 9-4 | John Egan | 25/1 | 77 | 72 | 84 |
| 5 | hd | Zeitgeist (IRE) | 3 | L M Cumani | 3 | 9-1 | L Dettori | 9/4F | 87 | 81 | 93 |
| 6 | 4 | Barry Island | 6 | D R C Elsworth | 5 | 9-3 | Seb Sanders | 20/1 | 76 | 64 | 76 |
| 7 | 1¾ | Briareus | 7 | A M Balding | 4 | 9-4 | Ryan Moore | 7/1 | 77 | 62 | 74 |
| 8 | ¾ | Silvaline | 12 | T Keddy | 5 | 8-13 5 | Colin Haddon(7) | 10/1 | 79 | 63 | 75 |
| 9 | shd | Tender Falcon | 4 | R J Hodges | 4 | 8-7 | Frankie McDonald(3) | 14/1 | 69 | 53 | 65 |
| 10 | shd | Penzance | 5 | J R Fanshawe | 3 | 8-10 | J Murtagh | 7/1 | 82 | 66 | 78 |
| 11 | 3 | Feed The Meter (IRE) | 1 | T T Clement | 4 | 7-9 5 | Francis Ferris(3) | 20/1 | 57 | 36 | 48 |

**11 ran** TIME 2m 34.86s (slow by 4.86s) **TOTAL SP** 119%

SERGEANT CECIL more than made up for last week's flop in the Sandown race he won the year before, with connections reporting he had raced far too freely up with the pace under Kieren Fallon. The tactics could not have been more different here, as he was switched off at the back and raced from last to first in the final furlong, also edging right from the outside to the far rail. He remains high enough in the handicap but heads for Goodwood, with connections also eyeing the Tote-Ebor back over 14 furlongs, but he would be on the cusp of making the cut for that and has not shaped as though quite up to that task.

# GOODWOOD

27 July 2004

Good

### 4:25 Tatler Summer Season Stakes (Heritage Handicap) (Class B) (Class 2) (3yo+,0–105) 1m6f

[off 4:27] £29,000.00, £11,000.00, £5,500.00, £2,500.00, £1,250.00, £750.00

| | | | Draw | TRAINER | Age | Wgt | JOCKEY | SP | OR | TS | RPR |
|---|---|---|---|---|---|---|---|---|---|---|---|
| 1 | | Mephisto (IRE) | 16 | L M Cumani | 5 | 9-4 | Darryll Holland | 7/2F | 92 | 105 | 109+ |
| 2 | ½ | Sergeant Cecil | 3 | B R Millman | 5 | 9-1 | Jimmy Fortune | 16/1 | 89 | 101 | 99 |
| 3 | ½ | Jagger | 9 | G A Butler | 4 | 9-9 | Eddie Ahern | 9/2 | 97 | 109 | 107+ |
| 4 | ½ | Santando (GB) | 4 | C E Brittain | 4 | 9-2 v | K Fallon | 25/1 | 90 | 101 | 99 |
| 5 | ¾ | Self Defense | 1 | P R Chamings | 7 | 9-12 | J Murtagh | 25/1 | 100 | 110 | 108+ |
| 6 | 2½ | Big Moment | 6 | Mrs A J Perrett | 6 | 9-9 | L Dettori | 12/1 | 97 | 104 | 102 |

| | | | Draw | TRAINER | Age | Wgt | JOCKEY | SP | OR | TS | RPR |
|---|---|---|---|---|---|---|---|---|---|---|---|
| 7 | ½ | **Fourth Dimension (IRE)** | 10 | D Nicholls | 5 | 8-9 | Adrian T Nicholls | 50/1 | 83 | 89 | 87 |
| 8 | ¾ | **Dorothy's Friend** | 13 | R Charlton | 4 | 9-0 | Steve Drowne | 11/2 | 88 | 93 | 91 |
| 9 | nk | **Bendarshaan** | 8 | M Johnston | 4 | 8-13 | K Dalgleish | 14/1 | 87 | 91 | 89+ |
| 10 | shd | **Nawamees (IRE)** | 2 | G L Moore | 6 | 9-2 p | Ryan Moore | 33/1 | 90 | 94 | 92 |
| 11 | ½ | **Mamcazma** | 11 | D Morris | 6 | 9-2 | Michael Tebbutt | 25/1 | 90 | 94 | 91+ |
| 12 | 1½ | **Almah (SAF)** | 15 | Miss Venetia Williams | 6 | 9-2 | Robert Winston | 100/1 | 90 | 91 | 89 |
| 13 | 12 | **Hambleden** | 5 | M A Jarvis | 7 | 9-10 | Philip Robinson | 11/1 | 98 | 82 | 81 |
| 14 | 9 | **Anticipating** | 14 | A M Balding | 4 | 8-11 | Martin Dwyer | 14/1 | 85 | 56 | 55 |
| 15 | 6 | **Morson Boy (USA)** | 12 | M Johnston | 4 | 9-4 | Joe Fanning | 7/1 | 92 | 54 | 54 |

**15 ran** TIME 3m 1.35s (slow by 1.85s) **TOTAL SP** 120%

Sergeant Cecil looked the winner when he burst to the front, but there was no disgrace in his defeat. Indeed, he probably ran the race of his life, for he has never won off a mark this high. With 8st 3lb he will be lucky to make the cut in the Ebor, however.

# HAYDOCK

4 September 2004

Good

## 2:05 stanleybet.com Old Borough Cup Stakes (Heritage Handicap) (Class 2) (3yo+,0–105) 1m6f

[off 2:06] £52,000.00, £16,000.00, £8,000.00, £4,000.00

| | | | Draw | TRAINER | Age | Wgt | JOCKEY | SP | OR | TS | RPR |
|---|---|---|---|---|---|---|---|---|---|---|---|
| 1 | | **Defining** | 1 | J R Fanshawe | 5 | 9-3 | J Murtagh | 11/1 | 98 | 54 | 111+ |
| 2 | ¾ | **Sergeant Cecil (GB)** | 7 | B R Millman | 5 | 8-12 | Steve Drowne | 10/1 | 93 | 48 | 102 |
| 3 | hd | **Sendintank** | 12 | S C Williams | 4 | 8-1 5 | Martin Dwyer | 7/1 | 82 | 37 | 91+ |
| 4 | shd | **Lochbuie (IRE)** | 3 | G Wragg | 3 | 8-5 | John Egan | 11/2J | 97 | 52 | 106 |
| 5 | ½ | **Millville** | 11 | M A Jarvis | 4 | 8-4 | Philip Robinson | 7/1 | 85 | 39 | 93+ |
| 6 | 1 | **Crow Wood (GB)** | 6 | J G Given | 5 | 9-0 | Kerrin McEvoy | 33/1 | 95 | 48 | 101 |
| 7 | nk | **Ski Jump (USA)** | 9 | R A Fahey | 4 | 8-0 v | Paul Hanagan | 25/1 | 81 | 33 | 87 |
| 8 | ¾ | **High Action (USA)** | 15 | Ian Williams | 4 | 8-9 t | Jamie Spencer | 12/1 | 90 | 41 | 95 |
| 9 | 2 | **Lodger (FR)** | 16 | J Noseda | 4 | 8-8 | Richard Hughes | 16/1 | 89 | 38 | 91 |
| 10 | nk | **Loves Travelling (IRE)** | 4 | L M Cumani | 4 | 8-9 | Darryll Holland | 11/2J | 90 | 38 | 92+ |
| 11 | nk | **Trance (IRE)** | 10 | T D Barron | 4 | 8-1 | Phillip Makin(5) | 100/1 | 87 | 35 | 88 |
| 12 | 3 | **Sahem (IRE)** | 20 | C J Teague | 7 | 8-3 | W Supple | 66/1 | 84 | 28 | 81 |
| 13 | shd | **It's The Limit (USA)** | 19 | Mrs A J Perrett | 5 | 8-11 | M J Kinane | 12/1 | 92 | 35 | 89 |
| 14 | 2 | **Dr Sharp (IRE)** | 8 | T P Tate | 4 | 8-1 | Jimmy Quinn | 25/1 | 82 | 23 | 76 |
| 15 | ½ | **Jorobaden (FR)** | 2 | C F Wall | 4 | 8-6 | Richard Mullen | 66/1 | 87 | 27 | 81 |
| 16 | nk | **Trust Rule** | 18 | B W Hills | 4 | 8-9 | Michael Hills | 25/1 | 90 | 29 | 83 |
| 17 | 1 | **Almah (SAF)** | 14 | Miss Venetia Williams | 6 | 8-6 1 | Robert Winston | 66/1 | 86 | 25 | 79 |
| 18 | ½ | **Bendarshaan** | 17 | M Johnston | 4 | 8-8 | Royston Ffrench | 66/1 | 89 | 26 | 80 |
| 19 | 1¼ | **Albanov (IRE)** | 5 | M Johnston | 4 | 8-13 | K Darley | 33/1 | 94 | 30 | 83 |
| 20 | 2½ | **Pushkin** | 13 | M Johnston | 6 | 9-10 | Stanley Chin | 100/1 | 105 | 37 | 91 |

**20 ran** TIME 3m 0.43s (slow by 2.43s) **TOTAL SP** 119%

The race was run to suit Sergeant Cecil who benefited from the drying conditions and came from behind to finish a good second. He has been improving all season and continues on the upgrade.

# DONCASTER

10 September 2004

Good To Firm

## 1:50 totepool Mallard Stakes (Handicap) (Class 2) (3yo+,0–110) (1m6f132y) 1m6½f

[off 1:51] £23,200.00, £8,800.00, £4,400.00, £2,000.00, £1,000.00, £600.00

| | | | Draw | TRAINER | Age | Wgt | JOCKEY | SP | OR | TS | RPR |
|---|---|---|---|---|---|---|---|---|---|---|---|
| 1 | | **Lost Soldier Three (IRE)** | 2 | L M Cumani | 3 | 8-1 | Nicky Mackay(3) | 5/2F | 97 | 70 | 106+ |
| 2 | 1¼ | **Sergeant Cecil (GB)** | 5 | B R Millman | 5 | 8-12 | Jimmy Fortune | 5/1 | 93 | 64 | 100+ |
| 3 | hd | **Fantastic Love (USA)** | 3 | Saeed Bin Suroor | 4 | 9-6 t | L Dettori | 9/1 | 101 | 72 | 108 |

| | | | Draw | | Age | Wgt | | SP | OR | TS | RPR |
|---|---|---|---|---|---|---|---|---|---|---|---|
| 4 | 2½ | Trust Rule (GB) | 13 | B W Hills | 4 | 8-10 1tp | Michael Hills | 33/1 | 91 | 58 | 94 |
| 5 | 2½ | High Action (USA) | 10 | Ian Williams | 4 | 8-10 1t | K Darley | 20/1 | 91 | 55 | 91+ |
| 6 | 1½ | Star Member (IRE) | 15 | A P Jarvis | 5 | 9-2 | Kerrin McEvoy | 12/1 | 97 | 59 | 95 |
| 7 | 1½ | Midas Way | 12 | P R Chamings | 4 | 9-0 | Eddie Ahern | 20/1 | 95 | 55 | 91 |
| 8 | 1½ | Heisse | 1 | D R Loder | 4 | 8-12 | Ryan Moore | 50/1 | 93 | 51 | 86 |
| 9 | 1 | Supremacy | 4 | Sir Michael Stoute | 5 | 9-10 | K Fallon | 20/1 | 105 | 62 | 97 |
| 10 | 1 | Santando | 9 | C E Brittain | 4 | 8-10 1v | R Hills | 25/1 | 91 | 47 | 82 |
| 11 | shd | Yoshka | 14 | M Johnston | 3 | 7-13 | Royston Ffrench | 4/1 | 92 | 47 | 82 |
| 12 | ¾ | Bourgeois | 7 | T D Easterby | 7 | 9-1 | Robert Winston | 50/1 | 96 | 50 | 85 |
| 13 | 4 | Highland Games (IRE) | 8 | J G Given | 4 | 8-10 1 | T Quinn | 20/1 | 91 | 40 | 75 |
| 14 | ¾ | Zibeline (IRE) | 6 | B Ellison | 7 | 8-10 3b | Dane O'Neill | 20/1 | 91 | 39 | 74 |
| 15 | nk | Salsalino | 11 | A King | 4 | 9-5 | J D Smith | 50/1 | 100 | 48 | 82 |

**15 ran** TIME 3m 3.90s (fast by 2.30s) **TOTAL SP** 119%

Sergeant Cecil ran a blinder, coming from well off the pace and staying on strongly to be nearest at the finish.

# ASCOT
### 26 September 2004
### Good To Firm

**4:20 totesport Ascot Final Fling Stakes (Heritage Handicap) (Class 2) (3yo+)** 1m4f

[off 4:21] £34,800.00, £13,200.00, £6,600.00, £3,000.00, £1,500.00, £900.00

| | | | Draw | TRAINER | Age | Wgt | JOCKEY | SP | OR | TS | RPR |
|---|---|---|---|---|---|---|---|---|---|---|---|
| 1 | | Fort | 9 | M Johnston | 3 | 7-13 | Nicky Mackay(3) | 16/1 | 88 | 91 | 106 |
| 2 | 2½ | Elusive Dream (GB) | 7 | Sir Mark Prescott | 3 | 7-13 4 | Jamie Mackay | 9/4F | 85 | 84 | 99 |
| 3 | 3 | Sergeant Cecil | 12 | B R Millman | 5 | 9-1 | Jimmy Fortune | 11/2 | 93 | 87 | 102 |
| 4 | 1¾ | Pagan Dance (IRE) | 14 | Mrs A J Perrett | 5 | 9-0 p | Ryan Moore | 15/2 | 83 | 98 |  |
| 5 | 1¼ | Grampian | 2 | J G Given | 5 | 9-10 | T Quinn | 25/1 | 102 | 91 | 106 |
| 6 | shd | Ovambo (IRE) | 5 | P J Makin | 6 | 9-8 | Fergus Sweeney | 33/1 | 100 | 89 | 104 |
| 7 | 1½ | Trust Rule | 4 | B W Hills | 4 | 8-12 tp | Michael Hills | 14/1 | 90 | 77 | 92 |
| 8 | ¾ | Top Seed (IRE) | 10 | M R Channon | 3 | 9-2 | Ted Durcan | 50/1 | 102 | 88 | 102 |
| 9 | 1¼ | Weecandoo (IRE) | 3 | C N Allen | 6 | 8-6 | G Carter | 50/1 | 84 | 68 | 82 |
| 10 | hd | Flotta (GB) | 13 | M R Channon | 5 | 8-5 | Sam Hitchcott | 25/1 | 83 | 66 | 81 |
| 11 | 4 | Tawny Way | 6 | W Jarvis | 4 | 8-13 | Steve Drowne | 8/1 | 91 | 68 | 83 |
| 12 | 1¼ | Nawamees (IRE) | 11 | G L Moore | 6 | 8-10 p | Richard Hughes | 25/1 | 88 | 63 | 78 |
| 13 | 7 | Roehampton | 8 | Sir Michael Stoute | 3 | 8-11 v | K Fallon | 12/1 | 97 | 60 | 76 |
| 14 | 12 | Loves Travelling (IRE) | 15 | L M Cumani | 4 | 8-12 | L Dettori | 6/1 | 90 | 33 | 49 |

**14 ran** TIME 2m 32.38s (slow by 2.38s) **TOTAL SP** 121%

Sergeant Cecil, a course and distance winner in July, had since finished runner-up three times over 1m6f. Down in trip here, he made up a lot of ground from the rear, which must have been frustrating to connections, who may now consider stepping him back up in distance.

# EPSOM
### 20 April 2005
### Good To Soft

**3:05 bet@bluesq.com Great Metropolitan Stakes (Handicap) (Class 3) (4yo+,0-95)** (1m4f10y) 1m4f

[off 3:13] £12,391.69, £4,700.30, £2,350.15, £1,068.25, £534.13, £320.48

| | | | Draw | TRAINER | Age | Wgt | JOCKEY | SP | OR | TS | RPR |
|---|---|---|---|---|---|---|---|---|---|---|---|
| 1 | | Tender Falcon | 9 | R J Hodges | 5 | 8-7 | Sam Hitchcott | 20/1 | 82 | 76 | 95 |
| 2 | shd | Balkan Knight | 2 | D R C Elsworth | 5 | 8-8 | John Egan | 11/2 | 83 | 77 | 96 |
| 3 | 3 | Midas Way | 13 | P R Chamings | 5 | 9-2 | Seb Sanders | 14/1 | 91 | 80 | 100 |
| 4 | 4 | Bendarshaan | 10 | M Johnston | 5 | 8-9 b | K Darley | 3/1F | 84 | 66 | 87 |
| 5 | 2½ | Millville | 3 | M A Jarvis | 5 | 8-12 | Philip Robinson | 11/2 | 87 | 64 | 86 |
| 6 | 1 | Solo Flight (GB) | 8 | H Morrison | 8 | 8-13 | Ryan Moore | 16/1 | 88 | 64 | 85 |
| 7 | ¾ | Turbo (IRE) | 7 | T G Mills | 6 | 8-13 p | G Carter | 7/1 | 88 | 62 | 84 |
| 8 | 6 | Magnesium (USA) | 12 | B G Powell | 5 | 9-1 | T Quinn | 33/1 | 90 | 54 | 77 |

| | | | | | | | | | | | |
|---|---|---|---|---|---|---|---|---|---|---|---|
| 9 | nk | **Jeepstar** | 6 | T D Easterby | 5 | 8-9 | Micky Fenton | 14/1 | 84 | 47 | 71 |
| 10 | nk | **The Violin Player (USA)** | 11 | H J Collingridge | 4 | 8-9 | Darryll Holland | 10/1 | 85 | 48 | 71 |
| 11 | 8 | **Gavroche (IRE)** | 4 | C A Dwyer | 4 | 8-12 | J-P Guillambert | 40/1 | 88 | 37 | 62 |
| 12 | 1¼ | **Sergeant Cecil** | 5 | B R Millman | 6 | 9-5 | Alan Munro | 8/1 | 94 | 40 | 66 |
| 13 | 2 | **Prime Powered (IRE)** | 1 | G L Moore | 4 | 8-4 1 | Jimmy Quinn | 16/1 | 80 | 23 | 49 |

**13 ran** TIME 2m 43.18s (slow by 7.18s) **TOTAL SP** 123%

# NEWBURY
14 May 2005
Firm

**3:45 paddypower.com Stakes (Handicap) (Class 2) (4yo+,0-100)** (1m4f5y) 1m4f
[off 3:45] £13,212.40, £5,011.60, £2,505.80, £1,139.00, £569.50, £341.70

| | | | Draw | TRAINER | Age | Wgt | JOCKEY | SP | OR | TS | RPR |
|---|---|---|---|---|---|---|---|---|---|---|---|
| 1 | | **Flamboyant Lad** | 10 | B W Hills | 4 | 8-12 | Michael Hills | 2/1F | 90 | 51 | 101+ |
| 2 | 3 | **Sergeant Cecil** | 11 | B R Millman | 6 | 9-0 | Alan Munro | 8/1 | 92 | 48 | 98 |
| 3 | nk | **It's The Limit (USA)** | 9 | Mrs A J Perrett | 6 | 8-12 | J Murtagh | 20/1 | 90 | 46 | 96 |
| 4 | 2 | **Nordwind (IRE)** | 6 | W R Swinburn | 4 | 9-0 | L Dettori | 10/1 | 92 | 45 | 94 |
| 5 | 1¼ | **Bendarshaan** | 1 | M Johnston | 5 | 8-6 b | Joe Fanning | 11/1 | 84 | 35 | 84 |
| 6 | 3 | **Highland Games (IRE)** | 2 | L M Cumani | 5 | 8-11 | K Fallon | 7/1 | 89 | 35 | 85 |
| 7 | 5 | **Le Tiss (IRE)** | 12 | M R Channon | 4 | 8-7 | Ted Durcan | 8/1 | 85 | 23 | 73 |
| 8 | 1 | **Polygonal (FR)** | 8 | Mrs J R Ramsden | 5 | 9-2 | Jamie Spencer | 11/2 | 94 | 30 | 80 |
| 9 | 1½ | **Solo Flight** | 7 | H Morrison | 8 | 8-10 | Steve Drowne | 12/1 | 88 | 22 | 72 |
| 10 | nk | **Unavailable (IRE)** | 4 | M A Magnusson | 4 | 9-0 | Kerrin McEvoy | 33/1 | 92 | 25 | 75 |

**10 ran** TIME 2m 30.90s (fast by 1.10s) **TOTAL SP** 116%

Sergeant Cecil was trapped on the rails from 3f out and had to wait for Highland Games to give way before he could be extricated.
The winner was not going to be caught, but he stayed on well and took second well inside the final furlong. He wants a really strong gallop at this trip and will be suited by a return to 14 furlongs.

# EPSOM
4 June 2005
Good

**5:05 Vodafone Handicap (Class 2) (4yo+,0-100)** (1m4f10y) 1m4f
[off 5:10] £23,200.00, £8,800.00, £4,400.00, £2,000.00, £1,000.00, £600.00

| | | | Draw | TRAINER | Age | Wgt | JOCKEY | SP | OR | TS | RPR |
|---|---|---|---|---|---|---|---|---|---|---|---|
| 1 | | **Crow Wood** | 15 | J J Quinn | 6 | 8-10 | K Fallon | 9/2F | 88 | 100 | 102 |
| 2 | 2 | **Balkan Knight** | 4 | D R C Elsworth | 5 | 9-3 | John Egan | 13/2 | 95 | 104 | 106 |
| 3 | ½ | **Sergeant Cecil** | 20 | B R Millman | 6 | 9-0 | Alan Munro | 12/1 | 92 | 100 | 102 |
| 4 | 1¾ | **Camrose** | 9 | J L Dunlop | 4 | 8-13 | Jimmy Fortune | 25/1 | 91 | 96 | 98 |
| 5 | nk | **Millville** | 19 | M A Jarvis | 5 | 8-9 | Martin Dwyer | 10/1 | 87 | 91 | 94 |
| 6 | 1 | **Mocca (IRE)** | 10 | D J Coakley | 4 | 9-0 | L Dettori | 11/1 | 92 | 95 | 97 |
| 7 | 3½ | **Tungsten Strike (USA)** | 18 | Mrs A J Perrett | 4 | 9-7 | J Murtagh | 20/1 | 99 | 96 | 99 |
| 8 | nk | **Pagan Dance (IRE)** | 13 | Mrs A J Perrett | 6 | 9-1 p | M J Kinane | 14/1 | 93 | 89 | 92 |
| 9 | 2 | **Skylarker (USA)** | 12 | W S Kittow | 7 | 8-4 | Francis Norton | 25/1 | 82 | 75 | 78 |
| 10 | 1½ | **Tender Falcon** | 3 | R J Hodges | 5 | 8-9 | Sam Hitchcott | 5/1 | 87 | 78 | 80 |
| 11 | shd | **Gold Ring** | 16 | J A Geake | 5 | 9-2 | Dane O'Neill | 25/1 | 94 | 84 | 87 |
| 12 | hd | **Top Seed (IRE)** | 14 | M R Channon | 4 | 8-0 v1 | Edward Creighton(3) | 22/1 | 81 | 71 | 74 |
| 13 | 3½ | **Compton Drake** | 11 | G A Butler | 6 | 8-3 t | Adrian T Nicholls | 50/1 | 81 | 65 | 68 |
| 14 | nk | **Midas Way** | 17 | P R Chamings | 5 | 9-4 | Jimmy Quinn | 12/1 | 96 | 80 | 83 |
| 15 | 6 | **Nawamees (IRE)** | 8 | G L Moore | 7 | 8-9 p | Ryan Moore | 50/1 | 87 | 61 | 64 |
| 16 | 1 | **King's Thought** | 6 | S Gollings | 6 | 9-2 | Darryll Holland | 25/1 | 94 | 66 | 70 |
| 17 | 4 | **Sand And Stars (IRE)** | 5 | M H Tompkins | 4 | 8-3 | Chris Catlin | 33/1 | 81 | 46 | 50 |
| 18 | 8 | **Turbo (IRE)** | 1 | T G Mills | 6 | 8-8 | Shane Kelly | 33/1 | 86 | 37 | 42 |

| | | | | TRAINER | | Age | Wgt | JOCKEY | SP | OR | TS | RPR |
|---|---|---|---|---|---|---|---|---|---|---|---|---|
| 19 | 9 | **Pagan Sky (IRE)** | 7 | J A R Toller | | 6 | 8-7 | Lisa Jones | 14/1 | 85 | 20 | 27 |
| 20 | 11 | **Wait For The Will (USA)** | 2 | G L Moore | | 9 | 8-6 | Robyn Brisland | 100/1 | 84 | – | 8 |

**20 ran** TIME 2m 36.67s (slow by 0.67s) **TOTAL SP** 129%

Sergeant Cecil was another who came down the hill into Tattenham Corner in trepidation as he had done last time to lose ground on the front rank. He was also forced to race wide but picked up takingly into the final two furlongs. He continues to run fine races against some of the best handicappers around and back on a galloping track remains one to be placed in top handicaps.

# NEWCASTLE
25 June 2005
Good

### 3:15 John Smith's Northumberland Plate (Heritage Handicap) (Class 2) (3yo+) (2m19y) 2m
[off 3:16] £104,400.00, £39,600.00, £19,800.00, £9,000.00, £4,500.00, £2,700.00

| | | | Draw | TRAINER | Age | Wgt | JOCKEY | SP | OR | TS | RPR |
|---|---|---|---|---|---|---|---|---|---|---|---|
| 1 | | **Sergeant Cecil** | 7 | B R Millman | 6 | 8-8 | Alan Munro | 14/1 | 92 | 56 | 102 |
| 2 | 1½ | **Tungsten Strike (USA)** | 17 | Mrs A J Perrett | 4 | 9-1 | Joe Fanning | 16/1 | 99 | 61 | 108 |
| 3 | 1¼ | **Far Pavilions** | 11 | G A Swinbank | 6 | 9-0 | Robert Winston | 6/1 | 98 | 58 | 105 |
| 4 | shd | **Astrocharm (IRE)** | 1 | M H Tompkins | 6 | 8-11 | Saleem Golam(7) | 20/1 | 102 | 62 | 109 |
| 5 | nk | **Odiham** | 12 | H Morrison | 4 | 8-8 | Steve Drowne | 7/1 | 92 | 52 | 99 |
| 6 | nk | **Balkan Knight** | 20 | D R C Elsworth | 5 | 8-7 | Daniel Tudhope(5) | 16/1 | 96 | 55 | 102 |
| 7 | 1½ | **Sendintank** | 18 | S C Williams | 5 | 8-12 | David Allan | 33/1 | 96 | 54 | 100 |
| 8 | ¾ | **Mirjan (IRE)** | 13 | L Lungo | 9 | 8-9 b | Paul Hanagan | 25/1 | 93 | 50 | 97 |
| 9 | ½ | **Gold Ring** | 4 | J A Geake | 5 | 8-9 | Sam Hitchcott | 25/1 | 93 | 49 | 96 |
| 10 | ½ | **Cold Turkey** | 6 | G L Moore | 5 | 8-8 | Phillip Makin(3) | 33/1 | 95 | 50 | 97 |
| 11 | hd | **Swift Sailor** | 2 | M Johnston | 4 | 8-11 | K Darley | 7/2F | 95 | 50 | 97 |
| 12 | 1 | **Lochbuie (IRE)** | 8 | G Wragg | 4 | 9-10 | John Egan | 10/1 | 108 | 62 | 109 |
| 13 | ½ | **High Action (USA)** | 16 | Ian Williams | 5 | 8-8 | D Nolan(3) | 33/1 | 95 | 48 | 95 |
| 14 | 2 | **Star Member (IRE)** | 3 | Ian Williams | 6 | 8-10 | Paul Doe | 50/1 | 94 | 45 | 92 |
| 15 | 4 | **Pagan Dance (IRE)** | 10 | Mrs A J Perrett | 6 | 8-8 | Tony Culhane | 40/1 | 92 | 38 | 85 |
| 16 | 3 | **Tees Components** | 14 | K G Reveley | 10 | 8-8 t | Dean McKeown | 100/1 | 92 | 34 | 82 |
| 17 | nk | **Total Turtle (IRE)** | 9 | P F I Cole | 6 | 8-11 t | Fergal Lynch | 66/1 | 95 | 37 | 84 |
| 18 | shd | **Contact Dancer (IRE)** | 19 | M Johnston | 6 | 8-8 | Royston Ffrench | 33/1 | 92 | 34 | 81 |
| 19 | 29 | **Coconut Beach** | 15 | A P O'Brien | 4 | 8-9 | Seb Sanders | 8/1 | 93 | – | 47 |
| 20 | ½ | **Balyan** | 5 | J Howard Johnson | 4 | 8-8 | W Supple | 11/1 | 92 | – | 46 |

**20 ran** TIME 3m 29.37s (slow by 2.87s) **TOTAL SP** 127%

A high-class renewal, in effect a 92-108 handicap, run at a true gallop. SERGEANT CECIL never left the inside rail and met his fair share of traffic problems, but it may well have suited him as he has to be produced as late as possible. Having finally got an opening, he quickened between horses to lead inside the final furlong and stamina was certainly not a problem.

# GOODWOOD
26 July 2005
Good To Soft

### 4:35 Tatler Summer Season Stakes (Handicap) (Class 2) (3yo+,0-105) 1m6f
[off 4:39] £15,992.92, £6,066.28, £3,033.14, £1,378.70, £689.35, £413.61

| | | | Draw | TRAINER | Age | Wgt | JOCKEY | SP | OR | TS | RPR |
|---|---|---|---|---|---|---|---|---|---|---|---|
| 1 | | **Golden Quest** | 13 | M Johnston | 4 | 10-0 | Joe Fanning | 9/1 | 99 | 103 | 113 |
| 2 | shd | **Balkan Knight** | 1 | D R C Elsworth | 5 | 9-11 | K Fallon | 5/2F | 96 | 99 | 110+ |
| 3 | 1¼ | **Sergeant Cecil** | 12 | B R Millman | 6 | 9-11 | Alan Munro | 8/1 | 96 | 98 | 109 |
| 4 | 2½ | **Camrose** | 8 | J L Dunlop | 4 | 9-3 | Jimmy Fortune | 14/1 | 88 | 86 | 97 |
| 5 | 2½ | **Larkwing (IRE)** | 4 | G Wragg | 4 | 9-5 | Ted Durcan | 12/1 | 90 | 85 | 96 |
| 6 | 1½ | **Red Damson (IRE)** | 2 | Sir Mark Prescott | 4 | 9-3 | Seb Sanders | 7/1 | 88 | 80 | 91 |
| 7 | ½ | **Swift Sailor (GB)** | 6 | M Johnston | 4 | 9-12 | Darryll Holland | 11/2 | 97 | 89 | 100 |
| 8 | 3½ | **Pagan Dance (IRE)** | 5 | Mrs A J Perrett | 6 | 9-5 v1 | Ryan Moore | 33/1 | 90 | 77 | 88 |

| | | | Draw | | | | | | | |
|---|---|---|---|---|---|---|---|---|---|---|
| 9 | hd | **Big Moment** | 14 | Mrs A J Perrett | 7 | 9-13 | Shane Kelly | 14/1 | 98 | 84 | 96 |
| 10 | 2½ | **Vaughan** | 7 | Mrs A J Perrett | 4 | 9-9 | Jim Crowley | 25/1 | 94 | 77 | 88 |
| 11 | 15 | **Peak Of Perfection (IRE)** | 3 | M A Jarvis | 4 | 9-2 | Philip Robinson | 14/1 | 87 | 48 | 60 |
| 12 | 1½ | **First Ballot** | 10 | D R C Elsworth | 9 | 9-12 | John Egan | 25/1 | 97 | 56 | 68 |
| 13 | ¾ | **Star Member (IRE)** | 11 | Ian Williams | 6 | 9-7 | Jamie Spencer | 33/1 | 92 | 49 | 62 |

**13 ran** TIME 3m 3.34s (slow by 3.84s)   **TOTAL SP** 118%

Balkan Knight ought to be a factor in the Ebor, and so too should Sergeant Cecil, who was 7lb higher than when second here a year ago and so deserves plenty of credit for finishing so close. Rod Millman insists Sergeant Cecil is better on fast ground and a flat track, but York seldom favours horses ridden from so far behind as he and Balkan Knight were, so that's a worry.

# YORK

17 August 2005

Good

## 2:30 totesport Ebor (Heritage Handicap) (Class 2) (3yo+) (1m5f197y) 1m6f

[off 2:38] £130,000.00, £40,000.00, £20,000.00, £10,000.00

| | | | Draw | TRAINER | Age | Wgt | JOCKEY | SP | OR | TS | RPR |
|---|---|---|---|---|---|---|---|---|---|---|---|
| 1 | | **Sergeant Cecil** | 18 | B R Millman | 6 | 8-12 | Alan Munro | 11/1 | 96 | 89 | 109 |
| 2 | 1 | **Carte Diamond (USA)** | 8 | B Ellison | 4 | 9-7 | Jimmy Fortune | 20/1 | 105 | 97 | 116 |
| 3 | nk | **Grampian (GB)** | 2 | J G Given | 6 | 9-0 | T Quinn | 16/1 | 98 | 89 | 109 |
| 4 | ¾ | **Balkan Knight** | 7 | D R C Elsworth | 5 | 8-12 | John Egan | 9/2F | 96 | 86 | 106 |
| 5 | 2 | **Zeitgeist (IRE)** | 1 | L M Cumani | 4 | 9-0 v | Kerrin McEvoy | 10/1 | 98 | 86 | 105 |
| 6 | hd | **Jagger** | 4 | G A Butler | 5 | 9-2 | Darryll Holland | 16/1 | 100 | 87 | 107 |
| 7 | nk | **Sendintank (GB)** | 20 | S C Williams | 5 | 8-12 | Martin Dwyer | 12/1 | 96 | 83 | 103 |
| 8 | 2½ | **Odiham** | 5 | H Morrison | 4 | 8-8 | Steve Drowne | 25/1 | 92 | 75 | 95 |
| 9 | ¾ | **Waverley (IRE)** | 10 | H Morrison | 6 | 9-2 | Jamie Spencer | 20/1 | 100 | 82 | 102 |
| 10 | ½ | **Crow Wood** | 3 | J J Quinn | 6 | 9-1 | K Fallon | 8/1 | 99 | 81 | 100 |
| 11 | 2 | **High Action (USA)** | 16 | Ian Williams | 5 | 9-2 | Richard Hughes | 25/1 | 100 | 79 | 98 |
| 12 | nk | **Howle Hill (IRE)** | 15 | A King | 5 | 9-2 v1 | Ted Durcan | 100/1 | 100 | 79 | 98 |
| 13 | ¾ | **Millville** | 19 | M A Jarvis | 5 | 8-13 7 | Philip Robinson | 20/1 | 97 | 75 | 94 |
| 14 | 3 | **Defining (GB)** | 9 | J R Fanshawe | 6 | 9-10 | J Murtagh | 16/1 | 108 | 81 | 101 |
| 15 | ½ | **Star Member (IRE)** | 17 | Ian Williams | 6 | 8-8 | Seb Sanders | 50/1 | 92 | 65 | 84 |
| 16 | 2 | **Vaughan** | 14 | Mrs A J Perrett | 4 | 8-10 | Shane Kelly | 50/1 | 94 | 64 | 83 |
| 17 | hd | **Dubai Success** | 11 | B W Hills | 5 | 9-10 p | Michael Hills | 33/1 | 108 | 78 | 97 |
| 18 | 3½ | **Orpington** | 6 | D K Weld | 4 | 9-7 b | P J Smullen | 9/1 | 105 | 70 | 89 |
| 19 | 5 | **Swift Sailor (GB)** | 12 | M Johnston | 4 | 8-13 | K Darley | 25/1 | 97 | 55 | 74 |
| 20 | 5 | **Vinando** | 13 | C R Egerton | 4 | 9-1 t | Ryan Moore | 12/1 | 99 | 49 | 69 |

**20 ran** TIME 2m 54.56s (fast by 1.24s)   **TOTAL SP** 123%

SERGEANT CECIL, a proven hold-up performer, was given a balls-of-steel ride by Alan Munro, who sat in the back three horses until beginning a gradual forward move once in line for home. His progress was relentless and the further the race went, the stronger he became, and it was only a matter of whether he got a clear run entering the last, which he duly did, to settle the issue towards the finish.

A much-improved horse, who now goes into the history books as the first winner of both the Northumberland Plate and the Ebor in the same year since 1911, he is a credit to connections.

# DONCASTER

8 September 2005

Good

## 3:55 GNER Doncaster Cup (Group 2) (Class 1) (3yo+) 2m2f

[off 3:56] £58,000.00, £22,000.00, £11,000.00, £5,000.00, £2,500.00, £1,500.00

| | | | Draw | TRAINER | Age | Wgt | JOCKEY | SP | OR | TS | RPR |
|---|---|---|---|---|---|---|---|---|---|---|---|
| 1 | | **Millenary** | 7 | J L Dunlop | 8 | 9-4 b | T Quinn | 11/4 | 115 | 72 | 119+ |
| 2 | ¾ | **Sergeant Cecil** | 6 | B R Millman | 6 | 9-1 | Alan Munro | 6/1 | 104 | 68 | 115 |
| 3 | 1¾ | **Kasthari (IRE)** | 3 | J Howard Johnson | 6 | 9-1 | Philip Robinson | 16/1 | 112 | 66 | 113 |
| 4 | 1¼ | **High Action (USA)** | 1 | Ian Williams | 5 | 9-1 | Richard Hughes | 33/1 | 100 | 65 | 112 |
| 5 | 2½ | **Jagger** | 5 | G A Butler | 5 | 9-1 | Darryll Holland | 10/1 | 107 | 62 | 110 |

| 6 | 5 | **Distinction (IRE)** | 2 | Sir Michael Stoute | 6 | 9-4 | K Fallon | 5/4F | 115 | 60 | 108 |
| 7 | 29 | **Cover Up (IRE)** | 4 | Sir Michael Stoute | 8 | 9-1 | Ryan Moore | 11/1 | 104 | 24 | 76 |

**7 ran** TIME 3m 51.15s (fast by 2.85s) **TOTAL SP** 111%

Sergeant Cecil had made great strides this term and put in a career best effort to add to his victories in the Northumberland Plate and Ebor. He came through to lead a furlong out and battled onto the line and looks capable of making a bold effort to complete a remarkable treble in the Cesarewitch.

# NEWMARKET
15 October 2005
Good To Soft

**3:45 totesport Cesarewitch (Heritage Handicap) (Class 2) (3yo+)** 2m2f
[off 3:51] £75,400.00, £28,600.00, £14,300.00, £6,500.00, £3,250.00, £1,950.00

| | | | Draw | TRAINER | Age | Wgt | JOCKEY | SP | OR | TS | RPR |
|---|---|---|---|---|---|---|---|---|---|---|---|
| 1 | | **Sergeant Cecil** | 28 | B R Millman | 6 | 9-8 | Alan Munro | 10/1 | 104 | 108 | 116+ |
| 2 | ¾ | **King Revo (IRE)** | 1 | P C Haslam | 5 | 8-3 | Philip Robinson | 20/1 | 85 | 88 | 95 |
| 3 | 2 | **Inchnadamph** | 4 | T J Fitzgerald | 5 | 8-0 1t | Martin Dwyer | 50/1 | 82 | 83 | 90 |
| 4 | 2 | **Vinando** | 11 | C R Egerton | 4 | 9-3 tb | L Dettori | 25/1 | 99 | 98 | 105 |
| 5 | 3 | **Elusive Dream** | 10 | Sir Mark Prescott | 4 | 8-9 | Seb Sanders | 11/1 | 91 | 87 | 94 |
| 6 | 1 | **Land 'n Stars** | 22 | Jamie Poulton | 5 | 9-0 7 | Paul Doe | 9/1 | 96 | 91 | 98+ |
| 7 | hd | **Mirjan (IRE)** | 36 | L Lungo | 9 | 8-7 b | Paul Mulrennan(3) | 16/1 | 92 | 86 | 94 |
| 8 | nk | **Escayola (IRE)** | 9 | W J Haggas | 5 | 8-6 tb | John Egan | 16/1 | 88 | 82 | 90 |
| 9 | 2 | **Total Turtle (IRE)** | 23 | P F I Cole | 6 | 8-8 | N Callan | 100/1 | 90 | 82 | 90 |
| 10 | 1 | **Distant Prospect (IRE)** | 5 | A M Balding | 8 | 8-6 | Neil Chalmers(3) | 50/1 | 91 | 82 | 90+ |
| 11 | nk | **Quedex** | 18 | R J Price | 9 | 7-7 1 | Colin Haddon(5) | 50/1 | 80 | 70 | 78 |
| 12 | 1½ | **High Point (IRE)** | 7 | G P Enright | 7 | 7-12 2 | David Kinsella | 100/1 | 80 | 69 | 77 |
| 13 | 1¼ | **True Lover (GER)** | 20 | J W Mullins | 8 | 9-5 | Adam Kirby(5) | 100/1 | 106 | 93 | 101 |
| 14 | 2 | **Lets Roll** | 8 | C W Thornton | 4 | 7-13 31 | Saleem Golam(5) | 16/1 | 86 | 71 | 79 |
| 15 | ¾ | **Baddam** | 2 | J L Dunlop | 3 | 7-12 1 | Royston Ffrench | 16/1 | 92 | 77 | 85 |
| 16 | 3 | **Inchpast** | 13 | M H Tompkins | 4 | 7-12 b | Nelson De Souza(3) | 100/1 | 83 | 64 | 73 |
| 17 | nk | **Cordial (IRE)** | 17 | Sir Mark Prescott | 5 | 8-6 | Jamie Mackay | 66/1 | 88 | 69 | 77 |
| 18 | hd | **Bronwen (IRE)** | 34 | J Noseda | 3 | 7-12 6 | Jimmy Quinn | 33/1 | 92 | 73 | 81 |
| 19 | hd | **Odiham** | 3 | H Morrison | 4 | 8-10 v | Steve Drowne | 16/1 | 92 | 72 | 81 |
| 20 | 1 | **Swift Sailor** | 31 | M Johnston | 4 | 8-13 5 | Greg Fairley(5) | 11/1 | 100 | 79 | 88 |
| 21 | 6 | **Fortune Island (IRE)** | 16 | M C Pipe | 6 | 8-8 tv | Jimmy Fortune | 18/1 | 90 | 62 | 72 |
| 22 | ½ | **Calamintha** | 25 | M C Pipe | 5 | 7-12 3 | Lisa Jones | 50/1 | 80 | 52 | 62 |
| 23 | ¾ | **Master Wells (IRE)** | 6 | J W Unett | 4 | 7-10 | Duran Fentiman(5) | 150/1 | 80 | 51 | 61 |
| 24 | 3 | **Considine (USA)** | 27 | P Howling | 4 | 7-12 18 | Frankie McDonald | 200/1 | 80 | 47 | 58 |
| 25 | 2½ | **Ten Carat (GB)** | 33 | Mrs A J Perrett | 5 | 8-10 v1 | Richard Hughes | 20/1 | 92 | 57 | 67 |
| 26 | 6 | **Establishment** | 14 | C A Cyzer | 8 | 7-12 10 | Hayley Turner | 100/1 | 80 | 38 | 49 |
| 27 | 11 | **Highland Games (IRE)** | 12 | L M Cumani | 5 | 8-1 | Nicky Mackay | 66/1 | 83 | 28 | 41 |
| 28 | 3 | **Afrad (FR)** | 30 | N J Henderson | 4 | 8-11 | K Fallon | 3/1F | 93 | 34 | 48 |
| 29 | ¾ | **Sweet Indulgence (IRE)** | 26 | W J Musson | 4 | 7-12 1 | Dean Mernagh | 50/1 | 80 | 20 | 35 |
| 30 | 15 | **Tempsford (USA)** | 19 | Sir Mark Prescott | 5 | 9-1 5 | J-P Guillambert | 50/1 | 97 | 19 | 37 |
| 31 | 6 | **Penny Pictures (IRE)** | 29 | M C Pipe | 6 | 8-2 | Joe Fanning | 66/1 | 84 | – | 18 |
| 32 | 2½ | **Hippodrome (IRE)** | 32 | A P O'Brien | 3 | 8-3 1v1 | Eddie Ahern | 33/1 | 97 | 10 | 28 |
| 33 | 2½ | **Domenico (IRE)** | 21 | J R Jenkins | 7 | 7-9 420 | Jamie Jones(7) | 200/1 | 84 | – | 13 |
| 34 | dist | **The Last Cast** | 35 | H Morrison | 6 | 7-12 4 | Francis Ferris | 66/1 | 80 | – | – |

**34 ran** TIME 3m 54.79s (slow by 8.79s) **TOTAL SP** 139%

SERGEANT CECIL completed a unique treble of the Northumberland Plate, Ebor and this big handicap. He has proved himself a class act over staying trips this season and got into this race 5lb well-in, having been reassessed after his fine second to Millenary in the Doncaster Cup. He was given an ice-cool ride and benefited from staying close to the inside rail and taking the shortest way home, unlike some of his rivals. King Revo looked to have gone beyond recall as Sergeant Cecil waited for a gap, but he picked up strongly and won a shade cleverly.

# NEWBURY

22 April 2006

Good

## 2:10 Dubai Tennis Championships Stakes (Registered As The John Porter Stakes)
## (Group 3) (Class 1) (4yo+) (1m4f5y) 1m4f
[off 2:11] £28,390.00, £10,760.00, £5,385.00, £2,685.00, £1,345.00, £675.00

| | | | Draw | TRAINER | Age | Wgt | JOCKEY | SP | OR | TS | RPR |
|---|---|---|---|---|---|---|---|---|---|---|---|
| 1 | | Mubtaker (USA) | 11 | M P Tregoning | 9 | 9-1 | Martin Dwyer | 9/1 | 115 | 88 | 119 |
| 2 | nk | Munsef | 5 | J L Dunlop | 4 | 8-11 | T Quinn | 4/1 | 107 | 85 | 116+ |
| 3 | ½ | Maraahel (IRE) | 4 | Sir Michael Stoute | 5 | 8-12 | R Hills | 3/1F | 120 | 84 | 115 |
| 4 | 2½ | Sergeant Cecil | 10 | B R Millman | 7 | 8-12 | Alan Munro | 9/1 | 112 | 80 | 111 |
| 5 | ½ | The Whistling Teal | 1 | G Wragg | 10 | 8-12 | Steve Drowne | 16/1 | 115 | 79 | 110 |
| 6 | nk | Frank Sonata | 9 | M G Quinlan | 5 | 8-12 | Ryan Moore | 6/1 | 102 | 78 | 109 |
| 7 | 2 | Allexina (GB) | 8 | John M Oxx | 4 | 8-8 | M J Kinane | 15/2 | | 72 | 103 |
| 8 | 11 | Compton Bolter | 6 | G A Butler | 9 | 9-1 | C Soumillon | 28/1 | 110 | 60 | 105+ |
| 9 | ½ | Swift Sailor | 7 | G L Moore | 5 | 8-12 | Jimmy Fortune | 50/1 | 100 | 56 | 88 |
| 10 | 16 | Gulf (IRE) | 2 | D R C Elsworth | 7 | 8-12 | John Egan | 50/1 | 105 | 29 | 62 |
| 11 | 16 | Sri Diamond | 3 | S Kirk | 6 | 9-1 | Jamie Spencer | 10/1 | 98 | 4 | 40 |

**11 ran** TIME 2m 33.18s (slow by 1.18s) **TOTAL SP** 113%

Sergeant Cecil made a highly encouraging reappearance over a trip short of his best, coming with a steady run on the wide outside after being last still with under 3f to run. He will come on for the run and will have a live chance in next month's Yorkshire Cup.

# YORK

19 May 2006

Soft

## 2:45 Emirates Airline Yorkshire Cup (Group 2) (Class 1) (4yo+) (1m5f197y) 1m6f
[off 2:45] £79,492.00, £30,128.00, £15,078.00, £7,518.00, £3,766.00, £1,890.00

| | | | Draw | TRAINER | Age | Wgt | JOCKEY | SP | OR | TS | RPR |
|---|---|---|---|---|---|---|---|---|---|---|---|
| 1 | | Percussionist (IRE) | 4 | J Howard Johnson | 5 | 8-12 | Darryll Holland | 9/1 | 109 | 50 | 117 |
| 2 | 3 | Sergeant Cecil | 6 | B R Millman | 7 | 8-12 | Alan Munro | 9/2 | 112 | 46 | 113 |
| 3 | 6 | Orcadian | 5 | J M P Eustace | 5 | 8-12 | N Callan | 7/1 | 102 | 37 | 105 |
| 4 | 1¼ | Kastoria (IRE) | 10 | John M Oxx | 5 | 8-9 t | M J Kinane | 11/4F | | 32 | 101 |
| 5 | 6 | The Geezer (GB) | 9 | Saeed Bin Suroor | 4 | 8-12 | L Dettori | 7/2 | | 25 | 96 |
| 6 | 5 | Cherry Mix (FR) | 8 | Saeed Bin Suroor | 5 | 9-3 t | Kerrin McEvoy | 13/2 | | 23 | 94 |
| 7 | 134 | Winged D'Argent (IRE) | 7 | M Johnston | 5 | 8-12 | K Darley | 12/1 | 108 | — | — |

**7 ran** TIME 3m 12.41s (slow by 16.61s) **TOTAL SP** 110%

Royal Ascot beckons for Sergeant Cecil, who progressed remarkably through the handicap ranks last season and confirmed the promise of his reappearance to show he is worthy of respect in Pattern class, coming from off the pace to hold virtually every chance a furlong out and keeping on to come clear of the rest. His Cesarewitch victory shows he stays marathon trips and with no superstar such as Westerner in the race this year, he would have to feature high on any Gold Cup shortlist.

# ASCOT

22 June 2006

Good To Firm

## 3:50 Gold Cup (Group 1) (Class 1) (4yo+) 2m4f
[off 3:51] £136,953.36, £51,906.24, £25,977.24, £12,952.44, £6,488.28, £3,256.20

| | | | Draw | TRAINER | Age | Wgt | JOCKEY | SP | OR | TS | RPR |
|---|---|---|---|---|---|---|---|---|---|---|---|
| 1 | | Yeats (IRE) | 8 | A P O'Brien | 5 | 9-2 | K Fallon | 7/1 | | 109 | 123+ |
| 2 | 4 | Reefscape (GB) | 2 | A Fabre | 5 | 9-2 | C Soumillon | 100/30 | | 105 | 119+ |
| 3 | hd | Distinction (IRE) | 4 | Sir Michael Stoute | 7 | 9-2 | M J Kinane | 5/2F | 117 | 105 | 117 |
| 4 | 3 | High Action (USA) | 3 | Ian Williams | 6 | 9-2 | Richard Hughes | 100/1 | 101 | 102 | 114 |
| 5 | 1½ | Sergeant Cecil | 11 | B R Millman | 7 | 9-2 | Alan Munro | 5/1 | 111 | 100 | 112 |

| 6 | ¾ | **Guadalajara (GER)** | 12 | Saeed Bin Suroor | 5 | 8-13 | L Dettori | 12/1 | 108 | 97 | 109+ |
| 7 | 5 | **Barolo** | 7 | W R Swinburn | 7 | 9-2 | J Murtagh | 25/1 | 109 | 95 | 106 |
| 8 | nk | **Tungsten Strike (USA)** | 6 | Mrs A J Perrett | 5 | 9-2 | Ryan Moore | 8/1 | 106 | 94 | 106 |
| 9 | 19 | **Winged D'Argent (IRE)** | 5 | M Johnston | 5 | 9-2 | Joe Fanning | 33/1 | 108 | 75 | 85 |
| 10 | 3 | **Akarem** | 10 | K R Burke | 5 | 9-2 | Pat Cosgrave | 40/1 | | 72 | 81 |
| 11 | 129 | **Motafarred (IRE)** | 9 | Micky Hammond | 4 | 9-0 | N Callan | 200/1 | 75 | — | — |
| PU | | **Media Puzzle (USA)** | 1 | D K Weld | 9 | 9-2 b | P J Smullen | 16/1 | | — | — |

**12 ran** TIME 4m 20.45s (fast by 2.05s) **TOTAL SP** 116%

This obviously wasn't Sergeant Cecil's best form, but he lost a bit of momentum at a crucial stage through the incident on the home turn and can be rated a little better than the bare facts suggest. It's going to be hard for him this year, by the look of it.

# SANDOWN

8 July 2006

Good To Firm

### 3:45 Addleshaw Goddard Stakes (Registered As The Esher Stakes) (Listed Race) (Class 1) (4yo+) (2m78y) 2m½f

[off 3:47] £15,898.40, £6,025.60, £3,015.60, £1,503.60, £753.20

| | | | Draw | TRAINER | Age | Wgt | JOCKEY | SP | OR | TS | RPR |
|---|---|---|---|---|---|---|---|---|---|---|---|
| 1 | | **Land 'n Stars** | 4 | Jamie Poulton | 6 | 9-3 | Paul Doe | 16/1 | 103 | 46 | 109 |
| 2 | nk | **Sergeant Cecil (GB)** | 3 | B R Millman | 7 | 9-0 | Alan Munro | 5/6F | 111 | 43 | 106 |
| 3 | 1½ | **Winged D'Argent (IRE)** | 2 | M Johnston | 5 | 9-0 | John Egan | 13/2 | 108 | 41 | 104 |
| 4 | 1¾ | **Barolo** | 5 | W R Swinburn | 7 | 9-0 | Ted Durcan | 9/2 | 108 | 39 | 102 |
| 5 | 42 | **Vinando** | 1 | C R Egerton | 5 | 9-0 tb | Jamie Spencer | 5/1 | 103 | — | 51 |

**5 ran** TIME 3m 39.72s (slow by 6.32s) **TOTAL SP** 108%

Sergeant Cecil, who went into this race highest-rated but again found a small field and its slower tempo all against him after his thrilling big-handicap wins, where he was seemingly flying through late off fierce paces. Last year's *Racing Post* horse of the year is certainly finding it hard, having had to step out of handicaps into Pattern races, and certainly has not been helped by some tactical races not playing to his strengths. He has also shown his best with some juice in the ground, and it looks on this showing that he has been overrated for his second to the mercurial Percussionist in the Yorkshire Cup.

# GOODWOOD

3 August 2006

Good To Firm

### 3:15 ABN Amro Goodwood Cup (Group 2) (Class 1) (3yo+) 2m

[off 3:15] £56,780.00, £21,520.00, £10,770.00, £5,370.00, £2,690.00, £1,350.00

| | | | Draw | TRAINER | Age | Wgt | JOCKEY | SP | OR | TS | RPR |
|---|---|---|---|---|---|---|---|---|---|---|---|
| 1 | | **Yeats (IRE)** | 8 | A P O'Brien | 5 | 9-10 | M J Kinane | 10/11F | | 106 | 126+ |
| 2 | 5 | **Geordieland (FR)** | 6 | J A Osborne | 5 | 9-5 | L Dettori | 16/1 | 108 | 95 | 116+ |
| 3 | 3½ | **Tungsten Strike (USA)** | 1 | Mrs A J Perrett | 5 | 9-8 | Martin Dwyer | 25/1 | 113 | 94 | 113 |
| 4 | 1½ | **Sergeant Cecil** | 3 | B R Millman | 7 | 9-5 | Alan Munro | 10/1 | 110 | 89 | 109+ |
| 5 | nk | **Baddam** | 9 | M R Channon | 4 | 9-5 | Ian Mongan | 33/1 | 99 | 89 | 108 |
| 6 | hd | **Land 'n Stars** | 12 | Jamie Poulton | 6 | 9-5 | Paul Doe | 25/1 | 111 | 89 | 108 |
| 7 | ¾ | **Reefscape (GB)** | 2 | A Fabre | 5 | 9-10 | Richard Hughes | 11/2 | | 93 | 112 |
| 8 | shd | **Bulwark (IRE)** | 7 | Mrs A J Perrett | 4 | 9-5 eb | Kerrin McEvoy | 25/1 | 98 | 88 | 108+ |
| 9 | 3 | **Balkan Knight** | 15 | D R C Elsworth | 6 | 9-5 | John Egan | 20/1 | 108 | 84 | 105+ |
| 10 | 3 | **Cover Up (IRE)** | 13 | Sir Michael Stoute | 9 | 9-5 | Ryan Moore | 20/1 | 108 | 80 | 100 |
| 11 | 3½ | **Golden Quest** | 14 | M Johnston | 5 | 9-5 | Joe Fanning | 9/1 | 112 | 76 | 96 |
| 12 | 1 | **High Action (USA)** | 11 | Ian Williams | 6 | 9-5 | Eddie Ahern | 50/1 | 110 | 75 | 94 |
| 13 | 2½ | **Ebtikaar (IRE)** | 16 | J L Dunlop | 4 | 9-5 | R Hills | 25/1 | 97 | 72 | 91 |
| 14 | 1½ | **Winged D'Argent (IRE)** | 10 | M Johnston | 5 | 9-5 | K Darley | 66/1 | 107 | 70 | 90+ |
| 15 | 20 | **Foreign Affairs** | 5 | Sir Mark Prescott | 8 | 9-5 | Seb Sanders | 16/1 | 111 | 45 | 66+ |

**15 ran** TIME 3m 21.55s (fast by 2.65s) **TOTAL SP** 129%

Sergeant Cecil deserves rating better than the bare form as he fell foul of the blocked rail early in the straight. He lost all momentum and, by the time he had recovered and found room, the race was over. He was back in top stride at the line and continues in top form. He fully deserves a success at this level and still looks capable of such, although this fast pace is a prerequisite.

# YORK

22 August 2006

Good To Soft

## 2:15 Weatherbys Insurance Lonsdale Cup (Group 2) (Class 1) (3yo+) (1m7f198y) 2m

[off 2:16] £70,975.00, £26,900.00, £13,462.50, £6,712.50, £3,362.50, £1,687.50

| | | | Draw | TRAINER | Age | Wgt | JOCKEY | SP | OR | TS | RPR |
|---|---|---|---|---|---|---|---|---|---|---|---|
| 1 | | Sergeant Cecil | 7 | B R Millman | 7 | 9-1 | L Dettori | 11/4F | 111 | 102 | 117 |
| 2 | ½ | Franklins Gardens | 3 | M H Tompkins | 6 | 9-1 | N Callan | 17/2 | 107 | 102 | 116 |
| 3 | 5 | The Whistling Teal | 2 | G Wragg | 10 | 9-1 | Steve Drowne | 16/1 | 110 | 95 | 110 |
| 4 | 4 | Bulwark (IRE) | 5 | Mrs A J Perrett | 4 | 9-1 eb | Kerrin McEvoy | 12/1 | 105 | 90 | 106 |
| 5 | 2½ | Baddam | 9 | M R Channon | 4 | 9-1 | Ian Mongan | 12/1 | 105 | 87 | 103 |
| 6 | 3 | Golden Quest | 1 | M Johnston | 5 | 9-1 | Joe Fanning | 9/2 | 110 | 83 | 99 |
| 7 | 8 | Tungsten Strike (USA) | 8 | Mrs A J Perrett | 5 | 9-4 | Martin Dwyer | 4/1 | 112 | 76 | 95+ |
| 8 | 20 | Winged D'Argent (IRE) | 4 | M Johnston | 5 | 9-1 | K Darley | 20/1 | 105 | 47 | 65 |
| 9 | 7 | Ebtikaar (IRE) | 11 | J L Dunlop | 4 | 9-1 | R Hills | 16/1 | 96 | 38 | 57 |
| 10 | 10 | High Action (USA) | 6 | Ian Williams | 6 | 9-1 | Richard Hughes | 40/1 | 109 | 24 | 45 |
| 11 | 5 | Kasthari (IRE) | 10 | J Howard Johnson | 7 | 9-1 | Tom Eaves | 28/1 | 108 | 17 | 39 |

**11 ran** TIME 3m 28.47s (slow by 3.97s) **TOTAL SP** 113%

They went a decent gallop which suited SERGEANT CECIL, who had met trouble in running in the Goodwood Cup on his previous start and showed his true colours here, held up in rear, ridden over two furlongs out but staying on well under pressure to lead inside the final furlong. He had not enjoyed the success of 2005 previously this term but he had been facing much stiffer opposition than last season and he is clearly a very smart stayer, likely to give a good account in the Doncaster Cup and Prix du Cadran this autumn.

# YORK

8 September 2006

Good

## 3:15 GNER Doncaster Cup (Group 2) (Class 1) (3yo+) 2m2f

[off 3:15] £56,780.00, £21,520.00, £10,770.00, £5,370.00, £2,690.00, £1,350.00

| | | | Draw | TRAINER | Age | Wgt | JOCKEY | SP | OR | TS | RPR |
|---|---|---|---|---|---|---|---|---|---|---|---|
| 1 | | Sergeant Cecil | 4 | B R Millman | 7 | 9-4 | L Dettori | EvensF | 111 | — | 118 |
| 2 | 1 | Alcazar (IRE) | 7 | H Morrison | 11 | 9-1 | Micky Fenton | 11/2 | 114 | — | 114 |
| 3 | 2½ | Baddam (GB) | 3 | M R Channon | 4 | 9-1 | Ian Mongan | 10/1 | 103 | — | 111 |
| 4 | 1¼ | Kasthari (IRE) | 1 | J Howard Johnson | 7 | 9-1 | Darryll Holland | 33/1 | 106 | — | 110 |
| 5 | 1 | Souvenance | 5 | Sir Mark Prescott | 3 | 7-12 | Jamie Mackay | 11/1 | 102 | — | 106 |
| 6 | 1¼ | Clara Allen (IRE) | 2 | John E Kiely | 8 | 8-12 | T P O'Shea | 7/1 | | — | 104 |
| 7 | 12 | Tungsten Strike (USA) | 8 | Mrs A J Perrett | 5 | 9-4 | Ryan Moore | 15/2 | 111 | — | 97 |
| 8 | 8 | Winged D'Argent (IRE) | 6 | M Johnston | 5 | 9-1 b | Joe Fanning | 25/1 | 102 | — | 85 |

**8 ran** TIME 3m 58.37s **TOTAL SP** 113%

Another highlight in the career of SERGEANT CECIL, last year's Horse of the Year, who can only have added to his fan-club this season. Here, hot on the heels of his course win in last month's Lonsdale Cup, he produced yet another heart-warming display. Held up as usual, he made steady headway from five furlongs out and was produced to lead over a furlong out. He went to his right after going on, but, given a few reminders to keep him up to his work, he was never going to be caught. Second to Millenary in this race last year, he more than deserved to go one better here, under a 3lb penalty.

# LONGCHAMP

1 October 2006

Good

### 1:05 Prix du Cadran Casino Les Princes Barriere de Cannes (Group 1) (4yo+) 2m4f

[off 1:04] £98,517.00, £39,414.00, £19,707.00, £9,845.00, £4,931.00

| | | | Draw | TRAINER | Age | Wgt | JOCKEY | SP | OR | TS | RPR |
|---|---|---|---|---|---|---|---|---|---|---|---|
| 1 | | **Sergeant Cecil (GB)** | 5 | B R Millman | 7 | 9-2 | L Dettori | 2/1F | | 65 | 120 |
| 2 | ¾ | **Shamdala (IRE)** | 2 | A De Royer-Dupre | 4 | 8-13 | C Soumillon | 9/1 | | 61 | 116 |
| 3 | ½ | **Le Miracle (GER)** | 1 | W Baltromei | 5 | 9-2 | D Boeuf | 11/4 | | 64 | 119 |
| 4 | 1½ | **Reefscape (GB)** | 3 | A Fabre | 5 | 9-2 | K Fallon | 100/30 | | 62 | 117 |
| 5 | 5 | **Petite Speciale (USA)** | 4 | E Lecoiffier | 7 | 8-13 | C-P Lemaire | 50/1 | | 55 | 109 |
| 6 | ¾ | **Alcazar (IRE)** | 7 | H Morrison | 11 | 9-2 | Micky Fenton | 7/1 | | 57 | 111 |
| 7 | 1½ | **Baddam (GB)** | 6 | M R Channon | 4 | 9-2 | Ian Mongan | 20/1 | | 55 | 110 |

**7 ran** TIME 4m 20.90s (fast by 0.10s)  **TOTAL SP** 112%

Despite the absence of Gold Cup winner Yeats, the first of six Group 1 races on the card looked well up to scratch, with more than half the field having shown the level of form that has usually been required to land the prize in recent years. That said, it turned into much less of a test at the trip than the Royal Ascot showpiece due to only a steady gallop, and those ridden up with the pace appeared to be at an advantage. Which means this was a tremendous effort by SERGEANT CECIL, who did not get anything like the run of the race, held up as usual and still in rear on the home turn. He was being pushed along early in the straight and looked to have done well to take third place entering the final furlong, but he picked up so strongly that he led 50 yards from the post and scored a shade comfortably. The seven-year-old has done nothing but improve over the past two seasons and, although his Doncaster Cup form gave him every chance here, the way he won suggests strongly he is still on the upgrade, quickening past a runner-up who was good enough to win a Group 1 race over 1m4f in the summer, and nothing else was able to get into the race from off the pace. The winner will do even better granted the stronger gallop which suits his come-from-behind style and he must go well in the Gold Cup next year. Although no match for Yeats in June, he was hampered on the home turn and has improved since.

# LONGCHAMP

22 October 2006

Good

### 3:10 Prix Royal-Oak (Group 1) (3yo+) (1m7f110y) 1m7½f

[off 3:09] £98,517.00, £39,414.00, £19,707.00, £9,845.00, £4,931.00

| | | | Draw | TRAINER | Age | Wgt | JOCKEY | SP | OR | TS | RPR |
|---|---|---|---|---|---|---|---|---|---|---|---|
| 1 | | **Montare (IRE)** | 6 | J E Pease | 4 | 9-1 p | O Peslier | 58/10 | | 77 | 116+ |
| 2 | snk | **Bellamy Cay (GB)** | 10 | A Fabre | 4 | 9-4 | S Pasquier | 67/10 | | 80 | 118 |
| 3 | 1 | **Sergeant Cecil (GB)** | 1 | B R Millman | 7 | 9-4 | Ryan Moore | 27/10 | | 79 | 117+ |
| 4 | ¾ | **Lord Du Sud (FR)** | 9 | J-C Rouget | 5 | 9-4 | I Mendizabal | 21/10F | | 78 | 116 |
| 5 | ½ | **Rising Cross (GB)** | 3 | J R Best | 3 | 8-6 | Martin Dwyer | 36/1 | | 75 | 114 |
| 6 | 2 | **Loup De Mer (GER)** | 8 | W Baltromei | 4 | 9-4 | D Boeuf | 25/1 | | 75 | 114? |
| 7 | hd | **Shamdala (IRE)** | 5 | A De Royer-Dupre | 4 | 9-1 | C Soumillon | 42/10 | | 71 | 111 |
| 8 | ¾ | **Soledad (IRE)** | 2 | G Cherel | 6 | 9-4 | F Spanu | 33/1 | | 74 | 113 |
| 9 | 4 | **Petite Speciale (USA)** | 11 | E Lecoiffier | 7 | 9-1 | T Jarnet | 30/1 | | 65 | 106 |
| 10 | 15 | **Frank Sonata (GB)** | 7 | M G Quinlan | 5 | 9-4 | T P Queally | 29/1 | | 49 | 94 |

**10 ran** TIME 3m 20.30s (slow by 1.80s)  **TOTAL SP** 122%

Held up as usual, Sergeant Cecil was ridden along over three furlongs out. Switched out from his position on the rails in the home straight, he got going late on but was unable to reel in the front two. With his style of running, there is always a danger of that happening and it would be no surprise to see him turn the tables on the two horses that beat him home here should they clash again next season.

*Note: racing record complete to the end of 2006.*

THE AUTHOR, STEVE DENNIS

# INDEX